MAKING TRADE POLICY
IN THE EUROPEAN COMMUNITY

Also by J. P. Hayes

ECONOMIC EFFECTS OF SANCTIONS
ON SOUTHERN AFRICA

Making Trade Policy in the European Community

J. P. Hayes

St. Martin's Press

for the Trade Policy
Research Centre
University of Reading

First published in Great Britain 1993 by
THE MACMILLAN PRESS LTD
Houndmills, Basingstoke, Hampshire RG21 2XS
and London
Companies and representatives
throughout the world

A catalogue record for this book is available
from the British Library.

ISBN 0–333–58955–6

Printed in Great Britain by
Ipswich Book Co Ltd
Ipswich, Suffolk

First published in the United States of America 1993 by
Scholarly and Reference Division,
ST. MARTIN'S PRESS, INC.,
175 Fifth Avenue,
New York, N.Y. 10010

ISBN 0–312–09684–4

Library of Congress Cataloging-in-Publication Data
Hayes, J. P. (John Philip), 1924–
Making trade policy in the European Community / J. P. Hayes.
p.   cm.
Includes bibliographical references and index.
ISBN 0–312–09684–4
1. European Economic Community countries—Commercial policy.
2. European Economic Community countries—Commercial policy-
–Decision making.   I. Title.
HF1532.5.H39   1993
382'.3'094—dc20
                                        93–17297
                                        CIP

TRADE POLICY RESEARCH CENTRE

The Trade Policy Research Centre was established in London in 1968 to promote independent research and public discussion of policy issues in international economic relations. Its work has mostly focused on trade policies – broadly defined to embrace all policies, however described, that bear on the production structures of economies – and other trade-related issues. These policies, along with public finance, form the core of resource-allocation questions. How those questions are handled by governments is probably the main single influence on the wealth of nations.

The initiative in establishing the Centre came from Mr Hugh Corbet, who became the first Director, and Harry G. Johnson, who was part-time Director of Studies until he died in 1977. Among the founding members of the Centre's Advisory Board, later replaced by a Council, were Sir Roy Harrod, Professor Richard G. Lipsey, Mr W.G. Pullen (the first Chairman of the Council), Professor James E. Meade, Mr T.M. Rybczynski, Maxwell Stamp and Sir Eric Wyndham White.

Initially, the Centre was organised as an unincorporated association, but in 1978 it was incorporated as a company limited by guarantee. In 1990, the Centre's assets were acquired by Maxwell Stamp plc, economics and business consultants, with a view to carrying on the work through a new, and autonomous, company limited by guarantee. Early in 1993, the Centre was relocated at the University of Reading, outside London.

The principal function of the Centre is the sponsorship of research programmes and publications, including the Thames Essay series, on policy problems of both national and international importance. Seminars and other meetings are also held from time to time.

Publications are presented as professionally competent studies worthy of public consideration. The interpretations and conclusions in them are those of their respective authors and do not purport to represent the views of the Centre which, having general terms of reference, does not represent on any particular issue a consensus of opinion.

Enquiries should be addressed to the Director, Trade Policy Research Centre, University of Reading, Whiteknights Park, Reading, Berkshire RG6 2AA, United Kingdom.

Contents

Contents ix

List of Tables and Figures

Foreword

The trade policies of the European Community are of great importance both for residents of the Community and, given the Community's importance as a trading bloc, for the rest of the world. There
have been fears among its trading partners that, with the completion
of the internal market, the Community may turn in on itself and
become more protectionist in its dealings with the outside world.
Moreover, the Community – together with the United States, Japan
and others – plays a major part in the formulation and implementation of the rules of international trade laid down and arbitrated under
the General Agreement on Tariffs and Trade (GATT), as in the
Uruguay Round negotiations on the reform of the GATT trading
system, which were still in progress when this volume went to press.

The making of trade policy in any country is a complex process.
Trade policy is not like monetary policy which can be handed down
from on high. While certain general principles are employed, albeit
to varying degrees, trade policy usually represents a balance of
'grassroots' pressures from sectional interests, those wanting government intervention in the market process to protect, support or
otherwise assist their incomes.

Trade policy bears on the production structures of economies.
There was a time when the instruments of trade policy were border
measures – tariffs, quantitative import restrictions, anti-dumping
actions, subsidy-countervailing duties and para-tariff devices such as
customs-valuation procedures. Nowadays the instruments of trade
policy include measures which operate well inside a country's borders
and include public subsidies of various kinds, technical standards,
public procurement policies and other non-tariff measures that can be
used to discriminate against foreign suppliers in favour of domestic
ones. Non-tariff measures are frequently viewed as instruments of
industrial policy, which accordingly appears to be little more than a
euphemism for public support and protection. This study therefore
embraces industrial policy.

In the European Community, with twelve member countries, the
making of trade policy is much more complicated, even though it is
conducted at Community level. The founding Treaty of Rome lays
down that the Community shall operate a common commercial
policy. With the free movement of goods and services within the

Community, the maintenance by member countries of differential measures affecting imports would lead to non-Community goods entering the country through the other member countries maintaining the lowest barriers.

In spite of the efforts to establish common commercial policies in the European Community, it has proved difficult to put an end to national differences, as for example in arrangements affecting imports of textiles and clothing and motor vehicles. Questions arise at two levels. First, why do approaches to trade policy differ in different Community countries? Second, what are the processes by which common policies are agreed (or fail to be agreed) in the face of conflicting views and interests?

The actual process of making trade policy has been somewhat mysterious. For example, what is the relative influence of the Commission – the European Community's central executive body – and of the Council of Ministers, made up of representatives from the governments of member countries? What is the relative influence, at Community and national levels, of politicians inside and outside governments, of officials at various levels and of private interest groups? The author outlines, and attempts to judge between, various explanations of the policy-making process that have been put forward.

Commentators often see wide differences between policy as they consider how it should be conducted and how it actually emerges. Those who are involved in making trade policy, for their part, commonly accuse commentators of 'not living in the real world'. There is often a dialogue of the deaf. Part of the author's object has been to try to build bridges between practitioners and commentators, with suggestions for ways of improving the policy-making process in the future.

The volume is based on a number of case-studies. While, for reasons of length, the details of the case-studies could not be included in the volume, reference is made throughout to particular points which they demonstrate. For the most part, the underlying case-studies covered policies affecting imports of manufactured goods. The policies affecting trade in agricultural products, while they have been of central importance in the Uruguay Round negotiations, would require a book to themselves. (Policy-making issues over farm-support measures have been discussed in a separate study for the Trade Policy Research Centre by D. Gale Johnson, *World Agriculture in Disarray*, a revised edition of which was published in 1990.) Similarly, the question of export-credit policy raises technical questions which are of a different order to the questions covered in this volume.

The analysis focuses on the decade and a half 1977–92 when the conduct of trade policy was affected by two oil-price crises, an increase in worldwide inflation, a widespread rise in unemployment and increased competition from goods shipped from Japan and other countries in East Asia. These developments contributed to pressures for protection in the European Community and other developed countries. It is against this background that the influences which shape trade policy at both Community level and within member countries are examined here.

The author notes, almost in passing, that economists play little or no part in the making of trade policy in the European Community and concludes on the need for 'transparency' in the policy-making process. By transparency is meant not only visibility in the ways and means by which trade policy is conducted but also public knowledge of the effects – the costs and benefits – of measures being proposed or implemented. What is extraordinary about the conduct of economic policies in the European Community is that very little effort is made to assess the costs, in terms of the economy as a whole, of different policy options.

After an eminent career as a civil servant in the British Government and in various inter-governmental organisations, Mr Hayes undertook the study while a Senior Fellow at the Trade Policy Research Centre in 1984–89. The project was made possible by a substantial grant from the Ford Foundation in New York, a generous supporter of the Centre's work over the years.

The author acknowledges the comments of Martin Wolf who, as Director of Studies at the Centre, gave valuable help and encouragement in designing the study. Generous help was also received from various former trade ministers, from academic economists and political scientists and from officials and ex-officials of the Commission and national governments. Some of the officials, in particular, might not wish to be identified. Many of those who helped are acknowledged by references in the text and notes. The volume owes much of its final shape to the editorial labours of Thelma Liesner, when a Senior Editor at the Centre, but it goes without saying that responsibility for the correctness of the facts and judgements rests with the author alone.

As usual, it has to be stressed that the views expressed in the study do not reflect those of the Trade Policy Research Centre which, having general terms of reference, does not represent a consensus on

any particular issue. The purpose of the Centre is to promote independent research and public discussion of international economic
policy issues.

	HUGH CORBET
London	*Consultant*
December 1992	*Trade Policy Research Centre*

1 Importance and Complexity

The external trade policies of the European Community are important because of their impact on individuals both within the Community and in the outside world. But how are these policies made? By what influences are they shaped? There has been 'a lack of consensus concerning the nature of the political decision-making process' in matters of external trade policy, both in the European Community and elsewhere;[1] and the process of policy-making in a community of twelve countries is inevitably particularly complex.

Given the importance of the subject, it is highly relevant to ask a number of questions. To what extent have decisions in the Community in matters of external trade been shaped by ideas of national or Community well-being, and of the means considered necessary to secure the desired ends?[2] To what extent have they been influenced by sectional, bureaucratic and political interests, or by other pressures? What is the influence of institutional arrangements, both at Community level and within the member countries? The aim of this book is to analyse the ideas, interests and pressures that have shaped the Community's policies in matters of external trade.

In exploring these questions, the book concentrates for the most part on policies affecting imports of manufactured goods into the Community. It also concentrates on a fifteen-year period beginning in 1977. The starting date is significant as the point at which policies in the Community swung in a more protectionist direction, a reversal of the earlier post-war trend towards greater liberalisation of the import regime.

IMPORTANCE OF THE SUBJECT

The subject is of obvious importance, both for those who live in the European Community and for the rest of the world. For the inhabitants of the Community, trade policy has a major impact on the allocation of resources and, hence, on the general levels of prosperity in the countries which make up the Community. Moreover, trade policy is politically sensitive, since it affects the distribution of income and, more dramatically, who has a job and who is unemployed.

1

For the outside world, the trade policies of the European Community are of major importance both because of the great weight of the Community in international trade and because, together with the United States, it plays a major part in shaping the international trading system. Even leaving out of account the internal trade between the countries of the Community, the Community of twelve countries (that is, including Spain and Portugal, which became members at the beginning of 1986) took approximately 20 per cent of world imports of goods in each of the seven years 1984 to 1990. The figures suggest a gradually rising trend in the share of world imports, with the Community overtaking the United States of America as the world's largest importer in 1989 or 1990.[3]

The Community influences the international trading system by its own actions, by the pressures which it exerts on the policies of other countries and by its important role in the General Agreement on Tariffs and Trade (GATT) and elsewhere in influencing the rules governing international trade.

The Community's part in shaping the international trade regime has not escaped criticism. According to one author:

> Through its widespread recourse to protectionist and preferential arrangements of a kind which are incompatible with a liberal multilateral trading system, the Community has contributed to weakening not only the GATT but also the fundamental idea that international trade policies should be governed by a framework of accepted rules.[4]

ASPECTS OF EXTERNAL TRADE POLICY

A Common Commercial Policy

The Treaty of Rome, by which the European Economic Community was brought into being, lays down that the Community shall operate a common commercial policy. As regards imports, the need for a common external trade regime would, in any case, follow from the intention that the Community should form a true common market. With free movement of goods inside the Community it would make no sense for any member country to try to raise higher barriers than any other against imports from the outside world: its residents would tend to import these goods by way of the member country with the lowest barriers.

The Swing to Protectionism

Article 110 of the Treaty of Rome reads:

> By establishing a customs union between themselves the Member States intend to contribute, in conformity with the common interest, to the harmonious development of world trade, the progressive abolition of restrictions on international exchanges and the lowering of customs barriers[5]

In its early years the tendency in the European Commission, the central executive body of the Community, was to read this as an injunction to pursue liberal external trade policies.[6]

The Community has been a party to a series of negotiating rounds in the General Agreement on Tariffs and Trade (GATT), which agreed on progressive reductions of tariff protection. At the beginning of 1986, a year ahead of the agreed timetable, the Community completed the tariff reductions agreed in the GATT Tokyo Round negotiations. This brought chargeable rates of duty down to low levels (where duties are still charged) for most industrial goods (see Chapter 2).

As tariff protection has diminished in importance, and particularly from 1977 onwards, there has been increased emphasis on quantitative restrictions, and especially on voluntary restraint agreements concluded with exporting countries (including, in this category, restraints on textiles and clothing items under the international Multifibre Arrangement (MFA). In addition, the Community has secured protection by means of anti-dumping and anti-subsidy procedures. Two fairly recent articles have concluded that the Commission has been able to manipulate the estimation of dumping margins so as to be able to use anti-dumping procedures in considerable degree as a discretionary protectionist device.[7]

One topic of enquiry, then, will be why it is that the Community, having agreed to progressive reduction of protection by way of tariffs, has then decided to resort to other forms of protection on a significant scale. Why, it may be asked, have the policy-makers of the Community rejected the body of economic thought which suggests that liberal import policies, even on a unilateral basis, are the best policy. Do they reject the economic reasoning; or do they believe (rightly or wrongly) that it is worth keeping a certain amount of protection as a bargaining counter to exert pressure on other countries; or is it because policies are shaped by political or other influences?

Another manifestation of protectionism has been pressures to erect barriers against free movement within the common market of products of Japanese and other foreign investments in Community countries.

Some of the makers of trade policy would claim that this emphasis on protection is unduly one-sided. As already noted, the Community has participated in successive negotiating rounds in the GATT leading to liberalisation of international trade. Moreover, it is relevant to consider why the Community, if it has decided on or condoned protection against imports of some types of goods at some times, has also in many cases resisted lobbying for protection.

Another question: despite the pressures to agree on a common, Community-wide external trade regime, individual countries of the Community have obstinately retained their own quantitative restrictions on various imports, or restraint agreements, of varying degrees of restrictiveness. This has been possible because, under Article 115 of the Treaty of Rome, the Commission can authorise barriers against the importation of particular goods by way of other Community countries. The decision to 'complete' the single Community market by the end of 1992 has increased the pressure to install single, Community-wide import regimes for goods for which restraint agreements will remain in force. The question nevertheless remains why the Commission has had so much difficulty, over two decades, in securing a truly common external commercial policy for certain imports.[8]

The planned completion of the internal market also raises certain questions. Despite numerous reassurances by Community spokesmen, there have been fears in the outside world that increased competition within the Community might lead to greater protection against imports from the outside world – 'fortress Europe'. This, it is feared, might contribute to the division of the world into a number of trading blocs, each raising barriers against imports from the others, with loss of economic welfare and increased political tension. Examination of the influences shaping decisions in the past can help to illuminate the prospects for the future.

Other Policy Issues

Even leaving aside export promotion and export credit policy (not covered in this study), Community trade policy has been by no means exclusively concerned with protection of domestic producers or with the removal or denial of protection. Thus, for example, a major concern has been to ward off threats of protection against Community exports by other countries, and notably by the United States. The Community has put pressure on Japan to improve market access for Community goods, and to reduce its current account surplus, both bilaterally and overall. At the same time, it has reacted against threats that United States protection might lead to diversion of increased amounts of Japanese goods to the European market or that the United States might secure special privileges in the Japanese market at the expense of Community exporters. It wishes to see the more advanced of the developing countries progressively assume the full obligation of GATT membership. These are just some examples of the multifariousness of Community trade policies.

The Uruguay Round

Since the mid-1980s, the Community has had to decide its position, first on the launching of a new round of trade negotiations in the GATT and then on the many issues arising in the negotiations (generally known as the Uruguay Round). The scope of the Uruguay Round gives an indication of the breadth of the issues covered by the general rubric of trade policy. Major topics included in the round are:

(a) tariff protection
(b) policies affecting trade in agricultural products
(c) treatment of imports of tropical products
(d) rules governing subsidies and imposition of countervailing duties against imported goods adjudged to have been subsidised
(e) rules governing protection against goods adjudged to have been dumped – that is, exported at less than 'normal value'
(f) safeguard protection against upsurges of imports considered to be disruptive
(g) rules governing international trade in services
(h) rules governing trade-related investment measures
(i) dispute settlement in the GATT.

Since both the provisions of the Treaty or Rome and the logic of its existence as a common market determine that the Community should operate a common external trade policy, the Community has had to decide its agreed positions over the entire range of issues covered in the Uruguay Round.

Particular difficulties have arisen in the Uruguay Round over policies affecting international trade in agricultural products. The United States and other agricultural exporting countries complain that the mechanisms of the Community's Common Agricultural Policy (CAP) create unacceptable distortions in international trade. Due in large part to disagreements over agriculture, the Uruguay Round negotiations had still not been completed at the time of writing in the autumn of 1992, six years after the inauguration of the Round.

The political economy of agriculture, while it has been of central importance for the Uruguay Round, would demand a book in itself. The subject of trade in services would also require a separate study, given the wide variety of services involved and the particular problems that they raise. As stated at the outset, this book concentrates on policies affecting imports of industrial products. This subject is already broad enough in itself. The topics of the Uruguay Round most particularly involved are: tariff protection; subsidies and countervailing duties; anti-dumping measures; safeguard protection; dispute settlement.

AIMS OF THE RESEARCH

There were three main aims in undertaking this investigation. First, since residents of the Community may be affected in a significant, even in a major, degree by actions and policies in the field of trade, they have a legitimate right to enquire how decisions that affect them are reached. The voter has a right to know whether trade policies in the Community are based on any coherent view of the objectives of policy and of the means necessary to secure those objectives. If there is such a view, what is it and how was it formed? To what extent are trade measures shaped by political pressures? Who gains and who loses? And why?

Second, the study may influence, directly or indirectly, the thinking of practitioners – officials concerned in the making of trade policy in national governments and in the Commission, even ministers and Commissioners. At present, academics and other commentators commonly accuse the practitioners of failing to follow sound and coherent principles of policy, or of being unduly influenced by certain particular sectional interests. The practitioners commonly reply that the academics and other critics do not understand 'the real world'. There is pretty much a dialogue of the deaf. A major aim of the study is to contribute to a more constructive dialogue.

Finally, the book should be of interest to people outside the European Community who are affected by the Community's actions and policies and hence have a real and legitimate interest in them.

TWO CENTRAL QUESTIONS

Within these broad aims two sets of questions will be of major concern. The first has to do with how decisions on trade policy are made in the Community and who is more influential and who less in shaping these decisions. The second set of questions is concerned with why decisions come out as they do. In particular, what is the relative force of (i) ideas of the public or national good and of the relationship between desired ends and the necessary means, and (ii) self-interest of producers and other private groups, of politicians and of officials.

How Decisions are Made

The complexity of trade-policy formation in the European Community has given rise to a variety of interpretations. One view is that there is '. . . a tendency [in the Community] for trade policies to be determined in response to the demands of the most protectionist members'.[9] Or to spell out this view more fully:

> The explanation . . . seems to be that the more liberally-inclined countries are obliged to agree to tight Community control on imports in order to persuade countries like France and the United Kingdom not to resort to national trade restrictions.[10]

The author suggests that:

> In general, Germany, the Netherlands and Denmark are inclined to take a more liberal stance on Community trade issues than France, Italy and the UK, who have more frequently tended to

adopt a protectionist approach. These differences in national attitudes towards trade restriction appear to have persisted over
time . . .'[11]

(In 1992, officials in London see the United Kingdom as being in the
liberal camp, with the southern countries of the Community tending
to be more protectionist – though Spain, for example, has made
major efforts to open its markets.)

This sort of interpretation regards the making of trade policy as a
matter of negotiation between the member governments. This is in
accordance with formal procedures. The founding treaties[12] give the
Commission the power and responsibility to make proposals on matters of trade policy, but the power of decision is vested in the Council,
made up of ministers from the member countries. Despite the obvious interpretation in terms of negotiations between governments, it
will be necessary to examine alternative interpretations which suggest
that decisions may be made by coalitions of particular interests in
member countries and the Commission, or by small numbers of
individuals able to operate with considerable latitude.

Influences on Decisions: Ideas and Interests

The question of the relative influence on decisions of ideas and
interests was highlighted in a series of radio lectures by David
Henderson, Director of Economics and Statistics in the Organisation
for Economic Cooperation and Development (OECD) in Paris.[13] He
referred to the well-known dictum of John Maynard Keynes, the
eminent economist, in the concluding note to The *General Theory of
Employment, Interest and Money* that '. . . soon or late, it is ideas,
not vested interests, which are dangerous for good or evil'. Professor
Henderson went on to argue that government policies are widely
influenced by what he called 'do-it-yourself economics'.

> . . . there is no doubt that the policies of governments have been,
> and still are, strongly influenced by economic ideas. But, contrary
> to what Keynes assumed, these have not necessarily been the ideas
> of economists. Over wide areas of policy the judgements of politi-
> cians and their officials, as also of public opinion in general, have
> been and still are guided to a large extent by beliefs and percep-
> tions about the working of the economic system, and about
> national interests and the welfare of the community, which owe

little or nothing to the economics profession. In so far as the world is indeed ruled by economic ideas, these are often the intuitive ideas of lay people, rather than the more elaborate systems of thought which occupy the minds of trained economists.[14]

A possible reaction to these lectures is that they exaggerated the independent power of ideas – that actual reasons for economic policies lie in various interests and political pressures – and that the arguments used in advocating or explaining these policies are in fact camouflage or attempts at persuasion. The question is central to the understanding of policy formation and provides a central connecting thread throughout this study.

METHOD OF INVESTIGATION

The investigation has been based on:

(a) the general literature on trade policy and decision making in the Community;
(b) material in the press including, notably, *Agence Europe*;[15]
(c) documents by the Commission;
(d) statements of participants in the decision-making process; and
(e) interviews in Brussels, Bonn, Paris and London.

In the United Kingdom, a number of ex-ministers and senior officials, serving and retired, responded to a questionnaire on the importance of various factors shaping British attitudes to trade policy. Not least, a detailed study was made of a number of specific cases of trade policy

(a) the Community's role in the negotiation of the first extension of the Multifibre Arrangement in 1977;
(b) trade relations with Japan;
(c) protection of cars and consumer electronic products;
(d) negotiation of the Tokyo Round Subsidies Code;
(e) the 1982 carbon steel negotiation with the United States;
(f) anti-dumping and anti-subsidy measures;
(g) adoption of the New Commercial Policy Instrument of 1984.

Material from the case-studies is used to throw light on the subjects discussed.

LAYOUT OF THE BOOK

In the chapter which follows, there is a general review of the principal characteristics of the European Community's trade policy over the years from the formation of the Community. The institutional framework of Community policy-making is outlined in Chapter 3. This leads on, in Chapter 4, to a review of the literature on the analysis of policy making, both at Community and at national levels.

The central section of the book consists of chapters on the formation of positions on questions of trade policy in three of the largest countries of the Community, Germany, France and the United Kingdom (Chapters 6 to 8). To set the scene for these country chapters, the relevant features of the economic background in the 1970s and the first half of the 1980s are recalled in Chapter 5.

The next three chapters pull together the main threads of the study. In Chapter 9 the influence of strategically-placed individuals in the decision-making process is considered and is set against the view of Community policy-making as a matter of inter-governmental politics. In the following chapter, the influence on Community trade policy of political, bureaucratic and private sectional interests is examined, together with the international pressures which may have a restraining influence on protective tendencies. In Chapter 11, an assessment is made of various explanations of policy in terms of economic ideas and of considerations of the public or national good.[16]

The final chapter summarises the main influences on the way in which decisions on Community trade policy are currently made and puts forward some suggestions for improvement.

2 Principal Characteristics of Community Trade Policy

As background to the study as a whole, the general characteristics of the trade policies followed by the European Community from its formation up to the early 1990s are reviewed in this chapter. The topics considered are:

(a) the Community's external tariff, together with the various pre-ferential arrangements for countries outside the Community;
(b) quantitative restrictions and restraint agreements with supplier countries;
(c) anti-dumping and anti-subsidy measures;
(d) the New Commercial Policy Instrument adopted in 1984;
(e) Community policies towards the GATT;
(f) questions arising in relations with two major partners, Japan and the United States.

For greater detail than can be included here on the Community's trade policies at the beginning of the 1990s, see the GATT *Trade Policy Review; The European Communities* (1991), and subsequent reviews as they appear.

COMMON EXTERNAL TARIFF

The customs union of the original six countries forming the Community was completed in 1968, and the customs union embracing the United Kingdom, Ireland and Denmark in 1977. Over the years since the formation of the European Community, rates of duty under the common external tariff have been progressively reduced in successive rounds of negotiations under the auspices of the GATT. At the beginning of 1986 (a year ahead of the schedule originally agreed) the Community implemented the final stage of the tariff reductions negotiated in the Tokyo Round of multilateral trade negotiations which were completed in 1979.

The average *ad valorem* tariffs (for non-preferential imports) were progressively reduced from 12.5 per cent (for the six original

11

Table 2.1 Community tariff rates remaining at 12.5 per cent or more after full implementation of Tokyo Round reductions

Item	Tariff rate (%)
Agricultural products (some)	Up to 30; (many products subject to levies in lieu of or in addition to tariffs)
Footwear (some)	Up to 20
Textiles and clothing (some)	12.5–15.0
Organic chemicals (some)	13.0–19.2
Motor vehicles (some)	12.5–22.0
Most integrated circuits, radios, television receivers and video recorders	14.0
Chromium oxides and hydroxides	13.4
Embossed, etc. wall-coverings incorporating plastics	12.5
Vacuum flasks	13.0
Glass inners for vacuum flasks	12.5
Helicopters (some)	15.0
Slide fasteners (some)	14.0
Tableware, kitchenware, etc. of porcelain or china	13.5
Stainless steel tableware	17.0

Source: *Integrated Tariff of the United Kingdom* (London: Her Majesty's Stationery Office, 1989).

Community countries) in 1958 to 7.3 per cent (simple average) or 5.1 per cent (trade-weighted average) in 1988. The simple average was 6.4 per cent for industrial goods and 12.4 per cent for agricultural products. Roughly 29 per cent of items were free of duty, 25 per cent were charged at 0 to 5 per cent and 35 per cent at 5.1 to 10 per cent.[1] The remaining relatively high tariff rates (12.5 per cent or more) are fairly highly concentrated in a few categories of goods though by no means all goods in these categories incur such high rates of duty. The categories in question are: agricultural products;[2] footwear; textiles and clothing; organic chemicals; some types of motor vehicle; some consumer electronic goods and electronic components. There are comparatively few rates of duty of 12.5 per cent or more on goods outside these categories (see Table 2.1).[3]

Preferential Arrangements

A particular feature of the Community's common external trade policy in the early days of the Community was a network of preferential tariff arrangements for Community trade in manufactures with the countries of the European Free Trade Association (EFTA),[4] with Mediterranean countries and with Asian, Caribbean and Pacific (ACP) countries under the successive Lomé Conventions.[5] In addition, a Generalised System of Preferences (GSP) for developing countries was agreed in the United Nations Conference on Trade and Development (UNCTAD) in 1971.

These preferential arrangements were made for political reasons. The United Kingdom and Denmark had been founder members of EFTA before they joined the Community. The Lomé Conventions reflect residual feelings of obligation of France and the United Kingdom to countries of their former colonial empires (although the Community refused to include the Asian countries of the Commonwealth under these arrangements). Special links with Mediterranean countries were designed to promote stability in this neighbouring area.

The preferences under these arrangements have become less significant over time, with the progressive reductions of the Community's common external tariff resulting from successive negotiating rounds in the GATT.[6] Moreover, preferences for certain 'sensitive' agricultural and manufactured products have been denied *ab initio*, or limited by ceilings on the quantity of goods qualifying for preferential access. Subsequently, export restraint arrangements have been negotiated with preferential partners, notably for textiles, clothing and steel. The preferential arrangements involve varying degrees of reciprocity.

The Community grants preferences to developing countries, other than those covered by the Lomé Convention, under the GSP. Many agricultural products and some manufactures are, however, excluded from the Community's GSP arrangements. For some 130 industrial products there have been quantitative limits to tariff-free access under the scheme. As in the Community's other preferential arrangements, the value to the beneficiaries of the GSP scheme has been reduced by the progressive reductions in the common external tariff.[7]

TRADE RELATIONS WITH EFTA

When the United Kingdom and Denmark joined the European Community in 1973, the Community entered into agreements with the remaining countries of EFTA for the progressive removal of tariffs and quantitative restrictions on trade in industrial (but not agricultural) products. Full implementation of the free trade agreements was achieved by the beginning of 1984. A joint ministerial meeting then declared the intention to extend the areas of economic cooperation. When, in 1985, the Community stated its intention of removing all remaining obstacles to the internal movement of goods and services by the end of 1992, there was concern in the EFTA countries that they would suffer from increased competition in the Community market. In January 1989, the President of the Commission extended an invitation to the EFTA countries to enter into new negotiations. (A motive on the side of the Community was to fend off pressures from EFTA countries to join the Community, so as to avoid possible difficulties to the deepening of Community cooperation.) Detailed negotiations were begun in June 1990 and completed in February 1992, with the aim of full ratification of a treaty on a European Economic Area (EEA) by the end of 1992. The treaty provides for removal of remaining barriers to most trade (though not for goods originating outside the EEA), and for free movement of services, capital and persons. There are special arrangements for agricultural products, fisheries, coal, energy and steel, and for such matters as passage of Community vehicles through the Alps. The EFTA countries agreed to accept the Community's rules on such matters as company law, consumer protection, research and development and social policy. While the EFTA countries cannot directly participate in the formulation of Community law, the agreement established machinery for consultation and settlement of disputes.

QUANTITATIVE RESTRICTIONS AND RESTRAINTS

With reductions of rates of duty under the common external tariff, the emphasis on protection of manufacturing in the Community has shifted to quantitative restrictions and restraint agreements with exporters (supplemented by anti-dumping and anti-subsidy measures).

Under the provisions of the Treaty of Rome, member countries were allowed to maintain some quantitative restrictions which were in force when the treaty was signed. In 1968, following formation of the customs union of the six founder members, the Council of Ministers adopted a common list of products imported without quantitative restrictions from contracting parties to the GATT outside the Community. A general rule was adopted that member states would abstain from introducing quantitative restrictions on products figuring in the common list. If, however, there were marked increases of imports into the Community of any such products or of total imports in conditions causing or threatening serious injury to Community producers, the Council could decide by weighted majority vote to withdraw products or exporting countries from the liberalisation list or, alternatively, to introduce Community quotas.[8] In addition, an individual member country could institute emergency import restrictions, but such restrictions must be notified immediately to the Commission for collective Community approval.[9] Between 1969 and 1974, the liberalisation list was progressively extended.[10]

The preamble to a Council Regulation of 1974 stated that experience had shown that trade practices may in certain cases call for a more expeditious protective procedure and the powers of the Commission in cases of emergency protection were therefore increased.[11] In 1976, a judgment of the European Court confirmed 'that the Community has had sole powers in commercial policy since the end of the transitional period' (31 December 1969).[12]

In 1982, the Commission made a breakthrough in the handling of quantitative import restrictions. The French and Italian governments had long resisted the greater transparency which would be involved in moving from a common liberalisation list to a list of products still subject to national quantitative restraints. In 1982, however, the Council finally agreed, 'in a desire for simplicity and greater transparency of import arrangements, . . . to draw up a list of quantitative restrictions still applicable at national level rather than a common liberalisation list'.[13]

Where quantitative restrictions are more severe for some Community countries than for others, they could be circumvented if it were possible to import by way of the countries with no restrictions, or less severe restraints, for the goods in question. Article 115 of the Treaty of Rome allows member states, with the approval of the Commission, to block such indirect imports. The Commission considers that Article 115 may be used only where there are formal import quotas, and not in support of voluntary restraint agreements or other such informal arrangements. By 1990, the number of restrictions in force had dropped to 112, 41 per cent by France, 29 per cent by Spain, 17 per cent by Italy and 10 per cent by Ireland. A great majority of these restrictions concerned textiles.[14] The Maastricht Treaty on European Union, signed in February 1992 subject to ratification by member governments, continues the provision for restraint of imports of particular items into individual member countries 'to ensure that the execution of measures of commercial policy taken in accordance with the Treaty by any Member State is not obstructed by deflection of trade, or where differences between such measures lead to economic difficulties in one or more Member States'. How this will be administered in practice was not clear at the time of writing.

The following paragraphs, on textiles and clothing, steel, cars and consumer electronic products, illustrate the complexity of the protective arrangements which developed in the 1970s and 1980s. Some, like the arrangements for textiles and clothing and steel, have been negotiated for the Community by the Commission. In other cases, notably cars, restraints have often been on a bilateral basis, nominally at least by inter-industry agreement.

Textiles and Clothing

For reasons which will be explored in subsequent chapters, a wide range of textile and clothing items have been among the goods receiving the highest levels of protection in Community countries. Table 2.1 shows that some items of clothing and textiles are subject to relatively high rates of duty under the common external tariff even after the full implementation of the tariff cuts agreed in the Tokyo Round of multilateral trade negotiations. In addition, there is a long history of quantitative restrictions and restraint agreements, with continuing differences in their severity as between the different countries of the Community.

In the 1960s, all the countries of the original Community of six countries maintained quantitative restrictions on broad ranges of textiles and clothing from Japan.[15] In 1969 the Community undertook a collective negotiation with Japan for an export restraint agreement for cotton textiles. This was the first-ever trade agreement between the Community as a whole and Japan, but there were still separate quotas for the individual Community countries. This agreement was negotiated under the Long Term Arrangement regarding International Trade in Cotton Textiles (LTA) of the GATT, an agreement covering a broad range of supplier countries, which had been instituted under pressure from the United States in 1962. The successor Multifibre Arrangement (MFA) was negotiated in the GATT in 1973 and went into effect at the beginning of 1974.

In the United Kingdom, an attempt to rationalise the cotton industry (not the first) under an Act of Parliament of 1959 was bolstered by inter-industry agreements for 'voluntary limitations' of exports to the United Kingdom from Hong Kong, India and Pakistan of cotton fabrics and made-up garments. This was supposed to give the textile industry a breathing space for two years. In the event, restraints, subsequently brought under the umbrella of the Community, were further tightened up.

When the LTA was replaced by the MFA at the beginning of 1974, the Community was slow to agree its position and enter into negotiations with supplying countries so that the full effects of the negotiated restraints were not apparent when discussions for the first extension of the MFA began in late 1976 and 1977. Under pressure in particular from France and the United Kingdom, the Commission secured agreement to a formula which would allow '. . . jointly agreed reasonable departures from particular elements [of the MFA] in particular cases'. This provided cover for negotiations with supplying countries allowing only minimal rates of growth for some items. Restraint agreements were negotiated not only with members of the MFA but also with Mediterranean countries benefitting from Community trade preferences. Once again, separate quotas were negotiated for individual Community countries.

At the next extension of the MFA, negotiated in 1981, the Community was interested in wording which would permit actual cuts in quotas for certain items from major suppliers. It was also concerned to be able to prevent surges of imports from supplying countries with under-utilised quotas. The Community has subsequently participated in further extensions of the MFA. There have also been, and remain, other restrictive arrangements with supplier countries not party to the MFA. The proposal under consideration in the Uruguay Round is to phase out quota restrictions under the MFA over a period of ten years.

With the intended removal of internal barriers in the Community after the end of 1992, individual country import quotas should disappear, remaining restraints being negotiated and administered on a Community-wide basis.

Steel

Steel is another product for which the Community has negotiated a number of restraint agreements. In response to pressure from the Community, the Ministry of International Trade and Industry (MITI) in Japan announced, in February 1972, voluntary restraints on steel exports as a second gesture of goodwill after the cotton textile agreement.

The scope of these restraint agreements was broadened following internal measures in the Community to regulate competition in the steel sector. In 1976 and 1977 the Community adopted internal guidelines for delivery and prices of steel products (the Simonet and Davignon Plans, named after the successive Commissioners responsible for industrial affairs). The Davignon plan was buttressed in 1978 by a number of anti-dumping actions against external suppliers and, within a short period, the principal suppliers agreed to export restraints.

In 1982, the Community in its turn was threatened with drastic reduction of its exports of steel as a result of a number of anti-dumping and anti-subsidy suits brought by steel producers in the United States. The Commission succeeded in negotiating an agreement which allowed continued exports of carbon steel from the Community to the United States under specified ceilings. On the other side of the balance, the Commission then put pressure on external suppliers of steel to accept further reductions in their exports to the Community. Brazil and other countries not previously covered by restraint agreements were, at this time, asked to agree to restrictions on their exports of steel and steel products. It appears that the number and coverage of restraint agreements for steel have been reduced on recent years, leaving some 10 arrangements in place at the beginning of the 1990s. These involved Brazil, three EFTA countries and several countries of eastern Europe.[16] In 1992 the Community imposed limits, under the terms of the bilateral association agreement, on imports of certain steel products from the Czech and Slovak Federal Republic. On the other side of the balance, Community steel exports were threatened by a further outbreak of anti-dumping applications in the United States.

Motor Vehicles

For motor vehicles, also, there is a history of quantitative restrictions and restraint agreements of differing severity for several Community countries, largely affecting imports from Japan.

The tightest restrictions have been imposed in Italy. Up to 1970, Italy totally prohibited imports of cars from Japan. Since this restriction ante-dated the coming into force of the Community's common commercial policy, Italy has been allowed to maintain quotas on imports of Japanese cars. In 1969, an agreement was reached to limit trade to 1000 cars per year. The Italian quota has subsequently been progressively increased. From 1986, Italy accepted some 2500 cars and 750 light commercial vehicles imported directly from Japan. According to authorisations by the Commission under Article 115, imports of Japanese cars by way of other countries of the Community were to rise from 14 000 in 1989 to 17 000 in 1990.[17] According to a report in the *Financial Times* of 2 May 1989, the Italian authorities had agreed that the quota limit would not be applied strictly to Nissan cars made in the United Kingdom.

Spain and Portugal have also been allowed to maintain quantitative restrictions on imports of motor vehicles. In 1991 Spain admitted 1000 cars and 200 commercial vehicles directly imported from Japan. The ceiling on imports from Japan by way of other countries of the Community was to increase from 5142 in 1989 to 7800 in 1990. In addition, Spain was authorised to limit indirect imports from South Korea to a maximum of 600, increased from 500 in 1989. In 1991 Portugal applied limits of 20 000 to passenger cars imported from outside the Community (excluding state trading countries). There were no importers bringing indirect imports of non-Community cars.[18]

Since 1975, the United Kingdom has had inter-industry agreements under which Japanese cars have been limited for most of the time to 10–11 per cent of the market. The French took steps in 1977 to limit Japanese cars to 3 per cent of their market.

The stated position of successive German governments has been against protection. In 1980, however, Count Lambsdorff, the German Economics Minister, proffered the Japanese 'friendly advice' on export restraints, particularly for cars.[19] In Japan, MITI subsequently announced a 'spontaneous' voluntary restraint agreement on exports to Germany of cars (and of colour television sets).

In February 1983, Commissioner Etienne Davignon negotiated a number of export restraints with the Japanese. For cars he announced agreement that 'the various limitations on the one or the other EEC national market will be respected and framed within the Community context'.[20] It is not clear what was meant by this last phrase. In fact, up to the recent past, the Commission has faced a major problem in any attempt to secure a common Community regime for imports of cars. In some countries of the Community there is no manufacture of cars, so the consumer interest is paramount; and, of the major car-producing countries, it has been seen that Italy, Spain and France (with Portugal) have been more restrictive in their attitude to imports than the United Kingdom and Germany.

From the beginning of 1993, the Commission intends to end all national restraints on imports of motor vehicles from Japan. In their place, an informal agreement was reached in 1991 by which the Japanese would limit exports to the Community as a whole, the intention being to remove all restraints by 1999.

Consumer Electronics

Another category of goods with a long history of quantitative restrictions and restraint agreements is consumer electronic products. Even up to 1990, differing restrictions for individual countries of the Community were in operation.

In 1962, France relaxed a total ban on imports of electronic goods from Japan, as part of a wider trade agreement. To secure this agreement, Japanese producers were obliged to enter into inter-industry agreements for electronic goods (as also for cotton textiles).[21] By contrast, restrictions in force in 1965 on imports of Japanese goods by Germany and Benelux were purely nominal.

In 1972, in response to various pressures from Community countries, MITI ordered a mix of export quotas and price increases for tape recorders, desk-top calculators and television sets for European markets. The German cartel office (*Kartellamt*) then declared such inter-industry agreements to be illegal distortions of the German market. Germany was accordingly omitted from the system of minimum prices administered by MITI and applying to Italy, the United Kingdom, Sweden, Finland, Ireland, Switzerland and Portugal. Controls were already in force on exports to Benelux and bilateral talks were in progress with France.

In January 1973, the Netherlands, without consulting its Community partners or the Commission, unilaterally stopped issuing import licences for electronic goods even though in principle the rules of the common external commercial policy had been in force since 1969. The Japanese then agreed voluntary restraints applying to Benelux as a whole. Pressure for an orderly marketing arrangement from the German electronics industry association was turned down by the Federal Government. The French electronics federation secured an extension of Japanese restraints on radios, record players, tape recorders and television sets. The Italian Government obtained Community approval for a 150 000 bi-annual quota on imports of tape recorders under Article XIX of the GATT (the safeguard clause). In his book on economic diplomacy between the Community and Japan, Albrecht Rothacher comments: 'Facing this pluralist diversity in national policies, Commission attempts to harmonise the Community's import policy on electronics had to fail, and so they did.'[22]

In 1974, the Japanese manufacturers agreed to a reduction of exports of colour television sets to the United Kingdom, in response to a marked drop in demand. In 1975, however, most Japanese restraints on exports of electronic goods to Europe were allowed to lapse, although the Japanese manufacturers gave a promise to consult in the event of market disturbance. France and Italy, however, continued to rely on quotas and voluntary restraint agreements.

The following year there were consultations between the United Kingdom and Japan on colour television sets and portable monochrome sets at both government and industry level. United Kingdom imports of portable monochrome television sets from all non-Community sources except state trading countries and Taiwan were already subject to surveillance arrangements. In July 1976, it was announced that all valid surveillance licences for imports from South Korea in the remainder of the year had been revoked. Imports of monochrome television sets from Taiwan were restricted with effect from 1 October 1976. (Until the end of 1977, the United Kingdom, Ireland and Denmark were permitted latitude in their commercial policies under the agreed transition period). In the early 1980s, United Kingdom producers agreed several restraint agreements with the industries in Japan, South Korea, Singapore, Thailand and Taiwan for various consumer electronic products. According to information available to the GATT secretariat, these arrangements were no longer in force in 1991.[23]

In 1977, the Italian Ministry of Foreign Trade introduced import licensing for Japanese audio equipment components (as well as heavy motorcycles) and then refused to process the licences. This was done, at least in part, in retaliation for Japanese restrictions on imports of silk yarn and ski boots. When bilateral discussions in the GATT ended in disagreement, the Commission requested the Italian authorities to free imports of audio components and to place a formal quota on motorcycles.

In October 1982, the French Minister of the Budget, Laurent Fabius, issued a decree that all video-cassette recorders imported into France should be routed through the small customs post at Poitiers, with the aim of slowing down the clearance of imports. The Commission promptly declared this to be illegal in that it applied to imports from other Community countries as well as from countries outside the Community.[24] The French Government was nevertheless able to maintain protective measures on video-cassette recorders: the

Poitiers decree was replaced by a system of advance declaration and statistical control of imports, allowing the foreign trade minister to stop 'excessive' imports of video-cassette recorders whenever he or she considered it appropriate.

Close on the heels of the Poitiers decree, Philips (Netherlands) and Grundig (Germany) lodged with the Commission a complaint alleging dumping of Japanese video-cassette recorders in Community markets. The allegation of dumping was never put to the test, however, since on his visit to Japan in February 1983 Commissioner Davignon secured agreement on quantitative restraints on exports of video-cassette recorders to the Community, and on minimum prices.

Later in 1983, Philips was the suppliant again, for protection for compact disc players. It was agreed to increase the rate of import duty, on a degressive basis, with compensation in the form of reduction of other states of duty as required by the rules of the GATT. In 1985, continued protection of video-cassette recorders also took the form of increased duty, with compensation.

Various quota restrictions and restraint agreements for electronic products were still in force in 1990 or 1991. In mid-1990, there were bilateral quotas authorised under Regulation 288/82 for various imports from Japan: for radios and television sets into France, Italy and Spain; colour television sets, transistors and integrated circuits into France and Italy; hi-fi radios, radio recorders and antennae into Italy; insulators into France. Japanese exports of video tape recorders and television tubes to France were still restricted under an industry-to-industry agreement. In addition, in 1989 France was authorised under Article 115 to restrict indirect imports of 13 electronic products (and Spain of two products). Denmark applied quantitative restrictions on insulated cables and wires from Taiwan. Spain, and to a lesser extent Portugal, applied quotas or non-automatic import licensing for a wide range of electrical and electronic products.[25]

In addition, in 1990 the Community accepted a minimum price undertaking for dynamic random access memory chips from Japan, with an anti-dumping duty of 60 per cent for supplies not conforming with the undertaking. A further anti-dumping action was in force for electronic weighing scales from Japan and electric motors from nine central and eastern European countries.[26]

Incidence of Quantitative Restrictions

The preceding paragraphs have traced the major developments in the protection of manufactures in the Community, but the coverage is

Table 2.2   Percentage of imports subject to quantitative restrictions, 1983

France	57.1
Belgium, Luxembourg	26.0
Netherlands	25.5
United Kingdom	14.3
Greece	13.4
Ireland	13.4
Germany	12.4
Denmark	11.7
Italy	6.9
Community average	22.3
For comparison:	
United States	43.0

Source: Julio J. Nogués, Andrzej Olechowski, L. Alan Winters, 'The Extent of Nontariff Barriers to Industrial Countries' Imports', *World Bank Economic Review*, vol. 1, no. 1 (Washington: September 1986).

Notes: The quantitative restrictions taken into account include voluntary restraint and 'orderly marketing' agreements (including those under the Multifibre Arrangement), as well as quantitative restrictions imposed by the Community or its member countries. They also cover import surveillance arrangements, variable levies (as for agricultural products), minimum price agreements, tariff quotas and anti-dumping and countervailing duties. They do not include measures applicable to all imports, or restrictions which may arise from government procurement practices, from technical or sanitary requirements or from regulations governing points of entry.

The figures refer to percentages of total imports subject to these various restrictions, measured at tariff line level, that is, the level of aggregation at which the restrictions are applied. They do not measure the extent of reduction of imports attributable to this collection of measures.

The authors note that weighting of the estimates according to the proportion of the affected items in total imports introduces a bias because of the effects of the barriers in restricting imports. Their estimates on alternative weighting systems designed to reduce this bias do not show, however, a significantly different overall picture.

not exhaustive. There are, for example, restraint agreements and other restrictions for other items including footwear, pottery and cutlery.

As has been seen, import restrictions are by no means uniform between Community countries in spite of the efforts of the Commission to bring about a truly common external trade regime. Table 2.2 shows differences in the percentages of imports of the various Community countries subject to quantitative restrictions in 1983 (on a broad definition including import surveillance arrangements, tariff quotas, and anti-dumping and anti-subsidy duties).

France was estimated to have by far the greatest incidence of quantitative restrictions in terms of percentage of trade in affected categories while in Italy, although the restraints were few in number, they were reported to be tighter than in other member countries.

Estimates by the Secretariat of UNCTAD suggest that the Community average for the import coverage of quantitative restrictions (on a similar, broad definition) increased by 14 per cent between 1981 and 1985, but then fell off slightly in 1986 and 1987.[27] The GATT *Trade Policy Review* points to the difficulty of making a judgement on the overall trend, in part because of lack of transparency in restraint agreements, but provides an overview of the situation at the beginning of the 1990s.

In mid-1990, individual countries of the Community still maintained several quantitative import restrictions (in addition to restraint agreements, recapitulated below). In France, 71 such restrictions were still in force, covering items including control instruments, clocks and watches, consumer electronics, transistors and integrated circuits. Italy maintained 48 such measures. All other member countries (excluding Spain and Portugal), together imposed less than ten residual restrictions.

The Community has made rather little use of Article XIX of the GATT, which makes provision for 'safeguard protection' against upsurges of imports judged to be disruptive. According to the apparent (but not undisputed) reading of the Article, such protection should be applied on a non-discriminatory basis, and exporting countries adversely affected by it have the right to seek compensation or take retaliatory trade measures. The three Article XIX measures maintained by the Community in 1990 set minimum prices for imports of various fruits, having been introduced in 1982, 1985 and 1989 respectively. In addition, Germany maintained one Article XIX action for coal imports, dating from 1958.

As has been seen, major restraints affecting imports into the Community of textiles and clothing items have been negotiated under the successive Multifibre Arrangements. In addition some 50 bilateral restraint arrangements were known to be in force at the time of the 1991 review, negotiated by the Commission for the Community as a whole, by individual member governments or by industry associations. The measures were mostly administered on the export side. Japan was the exporting country most involved, restraining or monitoring exports to the Community or to individual member countries of certain textile and clothing products, motor vehicles, household electrical and electronic equipment, machinery and metal flatware. Korean producers were also notably involved, with restraints, *inter alia*, on footwear and video cassette recorders. As noted above, the number and coverage of restraint agreements for steel appears to have been reduced in recent years.

ANTI-DUMPING AND ANTI-SUBSIDY MEASURES

Developments over time in the Community's anti-dumping and anti-subsidy activities are shown in Tables 2.3–2.5.

The apparent decline in the trend of the number of investigations initiated (Table 2.3) is largely due to an unusually large number in 1982 and unusually small numbers in 1989 and 1991. Certain more apparent trends emerge in the disposition of cases. There has, for example, been a marked decline in acceptance of price undertakings given by the exporting countries. There has been a notable decrease in findings of no dumping or no subsidisation, while findings of no injury have increased. A comparatively small number of investigations have been ended for 'other reasons', which include judgements that anti-dumping or anti-subsidy action would not be in the Community's interest. In total, one-third of cases disposed of in the twelve years 1980–91 ended without imposition of measures (definitive duties or price undertakings), the proportion being lower in 1980–3, higher in 1984–7, but with marked year-to-year fluctuations. Imposition of provisional duties has been higher in proportion to number of cases outstanding on average in 1987–9 than in the previous years. (Provisional duties may or may not be replaced by definitive duties or price undertakings.)

In the three years 1987 to 1989, there was a marked fall-off in the ratio of cases concluded to cases outstanding, leading to a rise in the number of investigations in progress; but in 1991 (as indeed in 1989) more investigations were concluded than were initiated.

In 1980–4, by far the leading product group for anti-dumping and anti-subsidy investigations was chemicals and allied products, accounting for over 40 per cent of all cases. However, by the years 1990–1 this group had been overtaken by iron and steel and other metals (nearly 30 per cent of cases) and mechanical engineering, electrical and electronic products (together accounting for 25 per cent

Table 2.3   Community anti-dumping and anti-subsidy cases in progress,
and their outcome
(number of cases[a])

	1980–83	1984–87	1988–91
Investigations initiated during period	169	148	130
Investigations concluded by			
imposition of definitive duty	45	26	65
acceptance of price undertakings	115	64	17
determination of no dumping	17	12	1
determination of no subsidisation	1	1	–
determination of no injury	21	26	29
other reasons	8	13	11
Total investigations concluded[b]	207	142	123
Provisional duties imposed	57	39	80

a. A case covers a single product or product group from a single importing
country, i.e. for a given product at any one time there may be a number of
cases involving different countries of origin.
b. Including investigations begun in previous period.

Source: Annual Reports of the Commission on the Communities' Anti-
Dumping and Anti-Subsidy Activities.

Table 2.4   Community anti-dumping and anti-subsidy investigations
initiated, by type of product
(number of cases)

	1980–83	1984–87	1988–91
Iron and steel	21	16	21
Other metals	12	5	15
Chemical products (and allied)	72	45	31
Electronics	30	32	14
Other mechanical engineering			19
Wood and paper	9	15	3
Textile and allied products	4	18	23
Other manufactures	21	17	4
Total	169	148	130

Source: As for Table 2.3.

Table 2.5 Community anti-dumping and anti-subsidy investigations, initiated by category of exporting country (number of cases)

	1980–83	1984–87	1988–91
OECD countries			
USA	22	3	1
Japan	9	14	14
Spain[a]	10	9	–
Turkey	2	6	12
Yugoslavia	7	16	9
Others[b]	14	12	4
Total OECD	64	60	40
USSR and Eastern Europe			
USSR	10	8	5
Eastern Europe	57	36	18
Total USSR and Eastern Europe	67	44	23
Developing countries			
Brazil	10	7	4
China	9	5	20
South Korea	1	7	14
Other newly-industrialising countries[c]	4	12	10
Other developing countries	14	13	19
Total developing countries	38	44	67
Total cases	169	148	130

a. Before accession to the Community.
b. Including Portugal before its accession to the Community. This group also includes South Africa.
c. Taiwan, Hong Kong, Singapore and Mexico.

Source: As for Table 2.3.

of cases). Despite trade restraints under the Multifibre Arrangement, cases for textiles and allied products climbed from 2 per cent of the total in 1980–3 to nearly a third of all investigations initiated in the two years 1989–90 (18 per cent of initiations over the longer period 1985–91). New investigations for all other items (wood and paper and 'other' in the table) declined sharply from an average of over 12 a year in 1982–5 to just under two a year in 1986–90.

In the four years 1981 to 1984, 46 per cent of investigations initiated concerned goods from the Soviet Union and Eastern Europe – not surprisingly, given the artificiality of export prices in these (then) centrally planned economies. However, the number of cases involving these countries then sharply fell away. Conversely, there has been a generally increasing trend in cases involving goods from China and countries generally described as newly-industrialising, and notably from South Korea. Cases involving United States exporters were 16 per cent of the total number in 1980–82, but thereafter slowed to a trickle. Cases on goods from Japan rose from one in each year 1980 and 1981 to an average of between three and four per year, around 10 per cent of total cases, in 1982–91. Nearly a quarter of cases in the whole period 1980–91 concerned goods from other OECD countries, notably Spain (before its accession to the Community), Yugoslavia and Turkey.

The Commission indicated that, in 1987, not more than 0.9 per cent of the Community's total imports of merchandise were subject to anti-dumping duties (excluding price undertakings). The authors of the GATT Trade Policy Review of 1991 nevertheless pointed out that:

> the uncertainty generated, and signals sent, by frequent resort to anti-dumping procedures are likely to affect larger volumes of trade. For example, there is evidence that, in view of possible anti-dumping action, trading partners have preferred to restrain voluntarily their exports to the Communities.[28]

In 1988, the Community attempted to prevent circumvention of anti-dumping duties through establishment of 'screwdriver plants' in the Community, assembling imported components. Council Regulation 2423/88 provided for the levying of duty on products thus assembled in the Community, where the like imported product was subject to an anti-dumping duty.

· In 1990, the Council of the GATT adopted a panel report which concluded that this regulation was in breach of the GATT rules, in particular in that the duties were internal charges in excess of those applied to similar domestic products, and that they amounted to treatment of imported products less favourable than that accorded to like products of national origin.

The Community has nevertheless continued to press for the regularisation under the GATT of this type of anti-circumvention measures, and has supported a clause to this effect in the Uruguay Round draft final act put forward by the director-general of the GATT in December 1991.

NEW COMMERCIAL POLICY INSTRUMENT

Under the 'New Commercial Policy Instrument' adopted in 1984, the Community has also taken powers, similar to these conferred on the President of the United States by Section 3 of the Trade Act of 1974, to take retaliatory action against non-Community countries if they are guilty (or are thought to be guilty) of illicit commercial practices. The purpose of these new powers is to make it possible for the Community to act immediately to deal with any such practices without waiting for the more long-drawn-out processes available under the GATT. It is specified that action should only be taken after failure to resolve the problem through the normal dispute settlement procedures. In fact, up to mid-1991 these powers had been used in only two cases.

COMMUNITY POLICY TOWARDS THE GATT

The Community's attitude to the GATT is somewhat ambiguous. It sees the rules of the GATT as valuable and prefers not to break them and it has taken a leading role in the various rounds of multilateral tariff negotiations. On the other hand, the Community has been by no means averse to 'bending' the rules, as may be shown by four examples.

First, many of the Community's preferential arrangements, while accepted *de facto*, could hardly be said to conform with the letter of the GATT.

Second, in the 1977 negotiations for the renewal of the Multifibre Arrangement, the Commission (responding to the demands of the United Kingdom and France) put extremely strong pressure on supplying countries, threatening to pursue autonomous measures, of highly doubtful legality under the GATT, if it did not secure the desired restraint levels in bilateral negotiations. By the time agreement was reached on the Protocol Extending the Agreement, the Commission had obtained all it had been instructed to obtain through the bilateral negotiations.

Third, in the Tokyo Round of multilateral trade negotiations, the

Community's aim was to secure the right to impose safeguard protection under Article XIX of the GATT on a source-selective basis. This would reduce the number, and probably also the economic strength, of the countries entitled to receive compensation or to take retaliatory measures under the terms of the article. While there exist subtle legal arguments that such selectivity is not inconsistent with Article XIX, such an approach is in clear opposition to the principle of non-discrimination which is central to the GATT. In 1990, in the course of the Uruguay Round negotiations, the Community has proposed a modified form of selectivity under the title of 'quota modulation'.

Fourth, for the Community (as for the United States) much of the protection up to the early 1990s has been achieved through restraint agreements with the suppliers, thus escaping GATT surveillance.

In general, the Community appears to value the GATT first and foremost as a restraint on actions by the United States which could be damaging (although it resists what it considers to be an unduly 'legalistic' approach to the GATT on the part of the authorities in the United States, preferring settlement through negotiation). The Community's trade relations with the remainder of the world outside Western Europe and North America are carried on largely outside the rules of the GATT – partial preferences on the one hand and bilateral restraint agreements on the other. The generalisation must, however, be qualified. For example, when in 1983 the Community decided on a temporary increase of the rate of duty on compact disc players from Japan, it followed the rule of the GATT by providing 'compensation' in the form of reduction of rates of duty on other items. Moreover, the Community, like the United States, wishes to use the Uruguay Round negotiations to put pressure on developing countries to reduce their protection of imports of goods and services.

TRADE RELATIONS WITH JAPAN AND THE UNITED STATES

It has been seen that many of the Community's acts of protection, including restraint agreements, have been against goods from Japan. The view in the Community (as in the United States) that trade relations with Japan raise particular problems will be discussed more fully in Chapter 11. In the Community's trade relations with Japan, however, there is an important triangular aspect, with the United States as the third angle of the triangle. Both the Community and the United States fear that protective actions by the other will result in unwelcome deflection of Japanese exports. Moreover, the Community is concerned that the United States may be able to exert greater pressure on Japan and so secure benefits to the detriment of Community interests.

A major concern of Community trade policy has been to counter threats from the United States to the commercial interests of the Community. These include action against Community products, both agricultural and industrial, found to have been subsidised. In the Tokyo round of multilateral trade negotiations, the Community negotiators successfully pressed the United States authorities to accept a test of 'material injury' before imposing countervailing duties on imports of goods found to have been subsidised. On the other hand, while the agreed Code 'recognize[s] that subsidies are widely used as important instruments for the promotion of social and economic policy objectives', there was no agreement on the dividing line between subsidies which would justify countervailing duties and those which would not.[29] The problem became important in 1982 when the United States authorities threatened to impose countervailing duties on a broad range of steel products from the Community. After intensive negotiations, the Community succeeded in substituting a restraint agreement on exports of bulk steel products to the United States.[30] Further adjustments of the rules on subsidies and countervailing duties have been on the agenda of the Uruguay Round.

Another Community concern has been with attempts by the United States to use extra-territorial legislation to prevent Community exports to the Soviet Union and Eastern Europe. At any one time over the past decade and more, the Community has been involved in a number of different trade disputes with the United States. Such disputes are nevertheless seen by many on both sides as potentially dangerous, not only economically but also politically within the framework of the North Atlantic Alliance. The political dimension in trade negotiations has been particularly strong in the case of the United States but relatively weak in relations with Japan.

MAJOR FEATURES OF COMMUNITY TRADE POLICY

This chapter has given a broad-brush picture of the evolution of Community trade policy up to the early 1990s, concentrating (as noted in Chapter 1) on policies affecting imports of industrial products. It has brought out certain major features of Community trade policy:

(a) the existence of the common external tariff and the progressive reduction of rates of duty;
(b) the continued desire of Community countries to protect certain types of manufactures, particularly through the use of restraint agreements with suppliers;
(c) the continuing failure, at any rate up to 1992, to put restraint agreements and some quantitative restrictions on imports onto a common, Community-wide basis;
(d) concern with averting or reducing protection by countries outside the Community;
(e) resistance to the development of a legalistic approach to the international regulation of trade policy through the development of case law in the GATT.

As a background to the attempt to explain how trade policy is made in the Community and to explore the major influences on policy, the Community's institutional framework is reviewed in the next chapter.

3 Institutional Framework of the European Community

Trade policy in the European Community is made in the framework of a written constitution laid down in the Treaty of Rome. For trade in coal and iron and steel, provisions of the Treaty of Paris, establishing the European Coal and Steel Community, may also apply. As part of this written constitution, the founding treaties established an institutional framework, which has been further shaped and developed with the passage of time.

The institutions to be considered in this chapter are:

(a) the Commission, the Community's central executive body which, under the treaties, has powers of initiative in matters of trade policy and which negotiates with other countries on behalf of the Community as a whole;
(b) The European Council of heads of government of the member states and the Council of Ministers (of varying composition) which have powers of decision in matters of trade policy;
(c) subordinate bodies of the Council, composed of national officials;
(d) the European Parliament, formerly an essentially consultative body though its powers in relation to internal Community matters were increased by the Single European Act, ratified in 1987;
(e) the European Court of Justice, the supreme arbiter in matters of Community law.

The nature and functions of these institutions will be considered in turn.

EUROPEAN COMMISSION

The Commission, with its powers of initiative and negotiation, has three layers. First there are the Commissioners and their President, political figures appointed by the member governments; second, there are the personal staffs of the Commissioners, *cabinets* in the French sense of the word; and third, a body of officials, answerable to the Commissioners.

33

In the Community of ten countries, there were 14 Commissioners, of whom two were appointed by the governments of each of the larger Community countries and one each by the smaller member countries. With the accession to membership of Spain and Portugal at the beginning of 1986, the number was increased to 17.

The Treaty of Rome laid down that the Commissioners are to be

> . . . chosen for their general competence and of indisputable independence. . . . The members of the Commission shall perform their duties in the general interest of the Community with complete independence. In the performance of their duties, they shall not seek or accept instructions from any Government or other body. (Article 157).

On taking up his office, each Commissioner takes an oath to this effect.

The Commissioners each hold one or more subject portfolios. At the same time, there is supposed to be a collective, collegiate responsibility for proposals put to the Council. The Commissioners are a heterogeneous group, however, and the leverage that can be exercised by the President of the Commission is somewhat limited, since he neither selects the other Commissioners nor has the power to dismiss them.[1]

Commission proposals which do not raise particularly controversial issues are distributed in writing for the approval of the various Commissioners. Some proposals are discussed in meetings of the Commissioners. Difficult questions may be put to the vote. How often this is done appears to depend on the approach of the President of the Commission at the time. In practice, matters of trade policy generally involve complex questions of detail and often have to be handled quickly, in the course of international trade negotiations. Thus Commissioners without direct responsibility for the questions at issue, and who are consequently not supported by advisers versed in the subject matter, tend to be at a disadvantage if they attempt to intervene.

Each Commissioner is supported, in his subject responsibilities, by the officials of the relevant Directorate-General of the Commission. In addition, each Commissioner has his own *cabinet* of personal advisers and aides.

The body of officials of the Commission with direct responsibility for matters of trade policy is located in the External Relations

Directorate-General (DG I). Two other Directorates have a major interest in trade policy, that is, DG III (Internal Market and Industrial Affairs) and DG VI (Agriculture).[2]

Of particular interest for the purposes of this study is the relationship between DG I and DG III. DG I is concerned with such matters as the reactions of trading partners and the rules of the GATT. DG III is more like an industry ministry in a national government, maintaining contact with industry representatives, understanding the problems of industries and tending, to some extent, to reflect their interests.

To deal with the overlapping and sometimes conflicting interests of the two Directorates, close if informal liaison has developed between them. Officials from each Directorate have been invited to meetings at all levels in the other, as required by the subject matter.

Powers and Responsibilities of the Commission

The founding treaties give the Commission broad powers and responsibilities. Specifically in relation to trade with the remainder of the world, the Treaty of Rome states:

> The Commission shall submit proposals to the Council for the putting into effect of this common commercial policy.
>
> Where agreements with third countries require to be negotiated, the Commission shall make recommendations to the Council, which will authorise the Commission to open the necessary negotiations. (from Article 113).

Clause 1 of Article 228 lays down that agreements between the Community and one or more States or an international organisation shall be negotiated by the Commission although the conclusion of the agreement is the prerogative of the Council after the European Parliament has been consulted. Clause 2 of the same article makes agreements concluded in this way binding on Member States.

A further article (Article 229) states that the Commission is be responsible for ensuring all suitable contacts with the organs of the United Nations, of their Specialised Agencies and of the GATT and, in fact, with all international organisations.

The Commission has strengthened its role in trade negotiations by building up an expertise, generally acknowledged, in the rules and procedures of the GATT. The Commission also administers the

Community's anti-dumping and anti-subsidy procedures, though on some points it is obliged to consult an advisory committee made up of officials from the member governments.

In general, according to one authority:

> the Commission is a great deal more than the Community's civil service. It administers the Common Market, the Common Agricultural Policy, and the whole range of internal agreements already reached. But it is also the Community's "think-tank" and its diplomatic service. It prepares a detailed agenda of work for the Council and drafts its legislation. It conducts, on behalf of the Community as a whole, complex relationships with the world at large. The Commission President plays a role, in European "Summit" meetings, on a par with the President or Prime Minister of a Member State.[3]

COUNCIL OF MINISTERS

While the Commission has the power and the responsibility to make proposals, the power of decision in most important questions of trade policy rests with the Council. As has been seen, Article 113 of the Treaty of Rome lays down that the Council 'will authorise the Commission to open the necessary negotiations'. The article further specifies that: 'The Commission shall conduct these negotiations . . . within the framework of such directives as the Council may issue to it.' Since, under the rules of the GATT, most matters of policy affecting imports involve negotiation with the partner countries affected, this provision gives the Council very broad powers in matters of trade policy.

The composition of the Council of Ministers was not specified in the Treaty of Rome. It consists of ministers from each member government; the national ministers making up the Council at any one time will be determined by the subject under discussion. The Council of foreign ministers was regarded as the top level of the Council hierarchy until the formation in 1974 of the European Council made up of heads of state or government. The Council of foreign ministers normally meets at least four times a year to review progress and to give high-level guidance.

Tacit agreement on procedures was reached after the first enlargement of the Community in 1973. Day-to-day matters, not agreed by officials, go to Council meetings made up of national ministers with the relevant subject responsibilities. Over the range of Community business as a whole, there are often Council meetings of one composition or another on several days of any given week. The Councils of sectoral ministers may request the Commission to redraft its proposals, but they should in principle do their utmost to reach agreement, referring disagreed points to the Council of foreign ministers only in exceptional circumstances. From the mid-1980s, discussions on trade policy have usually been on the agenda of the Council of foreign ministers although trade ministers may occupy the national chairs for discussion of trade matters. Alternatively, foreign ministers may be advised by officials from ministries of trade. The Council met at the level of trade ministers in March 1985 to agree positions for the launching of the Uruguay Round of multilateral negotiations. Moreover, Community trade ministers met at Punta del Este in the margin of the meeting there which launched the Uruguay Round and were present at the mid-term review meeting in December 1988 and the meeting originally intended to conclude the Uruguay Round in December 1990. In addition, the Spanish, when they held the presidency of the Community in the first half of 1989, called an informal meeting of trade ministers, and this practice has been followed under subsequent presidencies. These meetings, though, have no formal, policy-making status.

In 1974, a further tier was added to the Council structure by the establishment of the European Council, made up of the Presidents or Prime Ministers of the member countries. After the oil price increases of 1973–4 governments were concerned with national problems, and the difficulty of reaching agreement on Community matters greatly increased. The European Council (often referred to as the European Summit) was established with the idea of giving impetus to decision-making at the highest level.

Issues of trade policy have usually been settled at levels lower than the European Council, however, although it has made general declarations on trade policy.

Voting and the Luxembourg Compromise

The Treaty of Rome lays down that the Council shall exercise its powers in matters of trade policy by 'qualified' (that is, weighted) majority vote. Each country is given a number of votes according to its economic weight.

Before the accession of Spain and Portugal at the beginning of 1986, the votes of the ten member countries were weighted as follows:

Germany	10
France	10
Italy	10
United Kingdom	10
Belgium	5
Greece	5
Netherlands	5
Denmark	3
Ireland	3
Luxembourg	2
Total	63

For matters which the Treaty of Rome requires to be adopted on a proposal from the Commission, a qualified majority required 45 favourable votes. For other matters, there was the additional requirement that at least six (of the ten) member countries must vote in favour.

This voting requirement had certain important implications. In the first place, any two of the large countries (with ten votes each), could prevent a qualified majority; the smaller countries (less than ten votes each), if united, had 23 votes between them and to secure a qualified majority they needed the support of three of the four large countries. Second (and of substantial significance in the context of this study), 19 votes were needed to prevent the emergence of a qualified majority. Germany, the Netherlands and Denmark have often formed the liberal trade wing of the Community, combining in their wish to oppose or soften protective measures, but these three countries alone had a total of only 18 votes, one short of the number required to block a qualified majority.

Since their accession to the Community, Spain has had a voting weight of eight and Portugal of five. A qualified majority requires 54 votes, 23 votes being needed to block agreement.

The voting rules were qualified, in considerable degree, by the Luxembourg Compromise. This was agreed by the original six member states in January 1966, to bring to an end President de Gaulle's boycott of the Council. In effect, it gives a member country a power of veto if it declares that a 'very important' national interest is involved.

With the further enlargement of the Community to 12 countries, there were dangers that a strong presumption in favour of consensus would slow down decision-making still further and impede the effort to complete the unification of the internal market by 1992. The Single European Act, opened for signature in February 1986 and fully ratified in 1987, extends the rule of qualified majority voting, notably to most matters concerning barriers to internal trade (though with the important exception of harmonisation of national taxes). While this does not affect matters of the common external commercial policy, already subject in principle to decision by qualified majority vote, it may increase the presumption in favour of decision by qualified majority.

Subordinate Bodies of the Council

Matters requiring the attention of the Council are prepared by the Committee of Permanent Representatives (COREPER), which meets at the levels both of the national ambassadors to the Community and of their deputies, together with officials from the Commission. Agreements reached in COREPER go to the Council of foreign ministers as 'A' points which normally require no more than formal ratification. Matters not agreed in COREPER may be referred to a Council meeting made up of ministers with the appropriate subject responsibilities.

Another committee plays an important part in the making of trade policy; it is the Article 113 Committee, so called because a clause in Article 113 of the Treaty of Rome specifies that the Commission shall conduct trade negotiations with countries outside the Community 'in consultation with a special Committee appointed by the Council to assist the Commission in this task and within the framework of such directives as the Council may issue to it'.

While the role of the Article 113 Committee is nominally advisory, in practice this committee, consisting of officials with detailed knowledge of the issues and of the aims of their respective ministers, is an important link in the policy-making process (see Chapter 9).

EUROPEAN PARLIAMENT

The role of the European Parliament in matters of external trade policy is limited. The Single European Act considerably increased the powers of the Parliament to make its voice heard in such matters as agriculture, the Community's internal market, and regional and social policy, but gave no similar powers in relation to external trade. Association agreements with foreign countries have to be approved by the Parliament by absolute majority, but there is no such provision in relation, for example, to agreements reached in GATT negotiations.

The Parliament can nevertheless seek to influence trade policy, for example by adopting declarations, but these have only advisory force. One of the standing committees, the bodies through which a major part of the Parliament's work is done, is on external economic relations. Members of the Parliament can seek to influence policy by questions to the Commission, oral or written, which may give rise to debates. Indirect pressure might also be exercised through the Parliament's powers in relation to the Community Budget.[4] Finally, the Parliament has the power to dismiss the Commissioners *en masse* by a censure motion passed by a majority of two-thirds of the votes cast.[5] This, however, appears to be a weapon almost too drastic to be used, and it has been pointed out that the member governments could respond by promptly reappointing the same Commissioners.

EUROPEAN COURT OF JUSTICE

Not only have the European Communities their written constitutions in the form of the founding Treaties; there is also a Community 'supreme court', with powers to pronounce on what is legal and what is not under the Treaties. This imposes certain constraints on both the Commission and member governments. Cases may be brought before the European Court of Justice by the Commission, the European Parliament, member governments, nationals of Community countries or outsiders – for example, actions by Japanese producers against Community anti-dumping decisions.

The Court of Justice is charged under Article 164 of the Treaty of Rome with ensuring observance of law and justice in the interpretation and application of the Treaty. If the Commission considers that a member country has failed to fulfil any of its obligations, then it may refer the matter to the Court of Justice if, after the Commission has given a reasoned opinion, the country concerned does not comply with the terms of the opinion in the period of time laid down (Article 169). Similarly, a member country which considers that another member country has failed to fulfil any of its obligations may refer the matter to the Court of Justice after first referring any infringement of obligations to the Commission (Article 170).

In a case which was settled in the Court of Justice in 1964, the Court ruled that: ' . . . Community law within the sphere of competence of the Community, be it primary or secondary, is superior to Member State law even if the latter is subsequently enacted and/or of a constitutional nature'.[6] The reasoning behind the ruling of the Court was that member states had already limited their sovereign rights by the creation of the Community with its own institutions and legal capacity and they have thus 'created a body of law which binds both their nationals and themselves'.[7] Some member countries have had no difficulty in accepting this principle while others have accepted it with reservations.[8]

It may appear that the powers of the Court together with the provisions in the Treaty of Rome put the Commission in a strong position to implement a common commercial policy and to ensure that it is complied with. It has been pointed out, however, that the Court can exert only moral pressure.

One way in which governments can circumvent judgements of the Court is by delaying compliance until they have achieved the desired results.[9] Thus the role of the Court as an ally of the Commission in upholding the powers conferred by the founding treaties has been subject to certain limitations.

SUMMARY

This chapter might be summed up in the words, 'the Commission proposes, the Council disposes' – all within the framework of Community law as interpreted by the European Court. This suggests a view of decision-making in the Community as a matter of negotiation between governments, each with its internally agreed views on policy. It will be seen in the next chapter, however, that this is only one of a number of interpretations of how decisions in the Community are made.

4 Explanations of the Process of Decision-Making

Several differing views have been advanced of the nature of the decision-making process in the Community. One interpretation, that decisions on Community trade policy are shaped by negotiations between governments, raises questions at two levels: (i) how the desires and preferences expressed on behalf of the various member governments are arrived at and (ii) how agreement is reached on common Community policies.

Alternative interpretations have been advanced that decisions in the Community are often formed by particular coalitions of interests or by 'élite networks' consisting of limited members of individuals. These alternative models imply views on the behaviour of the national governments – that they either fail to decide their policy preferences or do not do all that is in their power to control or influence decisions at Community level. The questions of decision-making at the Community and the national levels are thus interlinked.

The voluminous literature on policy-making both within countries and in supra-national and international organisations suggests explanations of varying degrees of generality. Some contributions are concerned with the distribution of power and influence – whether influence over important decisions is concentrated in a few hands or widely dispersed. Others deal in greater detail with the determinants of political and bureaucratic behaviour. This chapter considers first the alternative explanations of decision-making at Community level and goes on to review a range of explanations applying at the national level.

DECISION-MAKING AT THE COMMUNITY LEVEL

In this first section, four 'explanations' of how Community policy is formed are examined. They are:

(a) inter-governmental politics;
(b) functionalism and neo-functionalism;

42

(c) transnationalism; and
(d) élite networks

Inter-governmental Politics

It was shown in Chapter 3 that proposals on matters of trade policy
are made by the Commission, but the power of decision lies with the
Council. Thus at first sight, at least, the making of trade policy in the
Community might appear to be a straightforward matter of inter-
governmental politics. On this view, national positions on questions
of trade policy are first decided within the governments of the various
countries and an agreed Community policy is reached, if at all, by a
process of bargaining among national ministers (or their representatives in official-level committees).

This explanation raises questions at two levels.

First, the ministers in the Council have been described as 'only the
tips of nine icebergs – nine [now twelve] national, totally independent, decision-making processes'.[1] It then has to be determined how
national governmental positions are reached and why they differ.
These issues will be explored in the chapters on the making of trade
policy in Germany, France and the United Kingdom. Second, there is
the question of how differing national views are compounded or
compromised into common Community policies. This also will be
considered in a later chapter.

In opposition to the view of decision-making as a process of inter-
governmental negotiation are the various alternative models which
suggest that Community policies are commonly formed by processes
which by-pass or circumvent the development of broadly agreed
views within national governments and the consequent need for
negotiation between established governmental positions.

Functionalism and Neo-functionalism

One alternative explanation of the decision-making process has been
labelled the functionalist approach and a variant of it, neo-functionalism. The functionalist explanation suggests that policy-making
in the Community is a problem-solving exercise in which common
interests are stressed, giving scope to the transaction of business by
technical experts.[2]

Carole Webb, a British political scientist, has criticised this particular explanation on the grounds that it fails to allow for the extent to

which Western European governments have become 'welfare agents' for interests within their countries.[3] In cases of difficulty, private interests turn to their national governments, which are drawn into the decision-making process as a political matter.

The 'neo-functionalist' explanation places greater emphasis on self-interest as the prime motivation of political activity and sees interest groups, bureaucracies and political élites as competing at the Community level. Whereas there is agreement among political élites on institutional arrangements and 'the rules of the game', divergences of interest within governments may allow the Commission to step in as allies of one departmental interest against others.

Transnationalism

A view intermediate between inter-governmentalism and neo-functionalism is described as transnationalism. Exponents of this view see the European Community as part of a world-wide economic interdependence in which governments, international institutions and non-governmental groups become closely and directly dependent on one another. They emphasise that some policy questions bring together particular groups of governmental and non-governmental participants, and policy decisions in some instances may be considerably influenced by Community-wide pressure groups or by coalitions of ministries from different countries.

Transnationalism, like neo-functionalism, thus raises the question whether governments are masters in their own houses. There are two ways in which Community decisions could escape the control of national governments.

(a) Governments could allow the Commission to make the decisions, possibly in consultation with representatives of private interests.
(b) Decisions could be made by agreement or negotiation between sub-units of national administrations, acting autonomously (possibly in cooperation with parts of the Commission and representatives of private interests).

It has been pointed out that:

For a transgovernmental coalition to take place, a sub-unit of one government must perceive a greater common interest with another government, or sub-units of another government, than with at least one pertinent agency in its own country; and central executive control must be loose enough to permit this perception to be translated into direct contacts with the foreign governments or agencies in question'.[4]

This is, perhaps, a little too black and white. Politics is the art of the possible, at Community as at national level. Importance attaches to what is negotiable. Thus a sub-unit of a national government may be able to argue that its preferred policy is negotiable, given the positions of its negotiating partners, while the policies advocated by other parts of the home government are not; or the representatives of one government may go out and look for allies for their preferred policy among the divided views within the other government machines. Nevertheless, 'the borderline between legitimate transgovernmental behaviour and treason may be unclear'.[5]

Élite Networks

A somewhat different set of Community policy-making models was proposed by an American political scientist, Glenda Goldstone Rosenthal.[6] She has made a conscious effort to apply three different models in each of a number of case studies. Her models were labelled:

(i) inter-governmental politics;
(ii) grass roots, interest group and parliamentary pressures; and
(iii) élite networks.

Professor Rosenthal concluded that explanation in terms of the activities of élite networks appeared to throw most light on decision-making in the Community. These 'élite networks' comprise groups within the bureaucracy which are prepared to mount a persistent and sustained campaign to achieve their ends. Highly specialised experts from different countries, who meet at regular intervals, come together in small committees and frequently confer by telephone.

Professor Rosenthal's interpretation, which might be described as an extreme variant of the neo-functionalist or transnational views, raises certain questions. First, to what extent did her research method, which relied heavily on interviews with selected, significant participants, lead to an exaggerated view of the contributions and freedom of action of certain individuals? Second, to what extent are policies influenced by representatives of particular private and bureaucratic interests, escaping more systematic and broadly-based decision-making within the various government machines? Third, where the influential figures are government representatives, are they able to operate according to their own personal views and preferences, so that the outcome depends on who happens to be in the right place (or the right hierarchical position) at the right time; or are their actions wholly or largely determined by a system of checks and balances, of penalties and rewards and by processes of indoctrination ('socialisation'), so that they act as the mouthpieces for policy positions based on a broad range of interests, considerations and pressures?

   This last question leads on to the national level where a number of aspects need to be considered including (i) the way in which national positions on questions of trade policy are formed; (ii) the degree of latitude or autonomy available to national representatives operating in Community bodies; and (iii) the pressures and influences which help to shape the exercise of any such latitude. Each of these will be considered in turn.

DECISION-MAKING AT THE NATIONAL LEVEL

A number of explanations of how decisions are arrived at by national governments have been put forward; three of these will be briefly considered. First, there is 'public choice' analysis, which investigates the consequences of the efforts of individuals to maximise their personal utility. Second, analysis of the 'public market for protection' reviews influences on the demand for protection and on the willingness of governments to supply it. Third, others emphasise the distribution of power and influence among different groups and the impact of these groups on governmental decisions.

Public Choice Analysis

Public choice analysis 'can be defined as the economic study of non-market decision-making, or simply the application of economics to political science. . . . The basic behavioural postulate of public choice, as for economics, is that man is an egoistic, rational, utility maximizer'.[7] In this explanation, government is seen as the monopoly producer of a wide range of collective, public goods (which include trade policy, with its positive or negative impact on various groups in the society). Individuals, as voters or through other means of influence, provide the demand for these public goods. Politicians and officials, as suppliers of public goods, may have scope to increase their individual 'utility' through varying degrees of monopoly or oligopoly power.

The public choice analysis is important because it attempts to build up a picture of the body politic as a whole, based on the motives of individuals and the interactions between them. It has been criticised, however, both on theoretical grounds and for yielding deductions which are falsified by the facts.[8] At the theoretical level, it is suggested that the assumption that all the participants seek to maximise something or other is without value because there is no way of knowing what it is they are seeking to maximise. Moreover, in the last resort, while everything is done by individuals, they do not operate in a vacuum. Their ways of apprehending the world are shaped by education, by reading and by exposure to the media as well as by professional and social contacts, and their decisions are influenced by the system of rewards and penalties within which they operate. Of course, there are rebels and independent thinkers, but they may be pushed aside or may be turned in time into passive conformists by repeated rebuffs and frustrations.

'The Political Market for Protection'

Related more or less closely to the public choice approach are the efforts which have been made to analyse the patterns of trade protection in various countries in terms of factors influencing the demand for and supply of protection. In a useful survey of work in this area,[9] Professor Robert Baldwin of the University of Wisconsin distinguishes seven major hypotheses or models:

(a) the common-interest or pressure group model, stressing the relative ability of different economic interests to organise political pressure groups;

(b) the adding-machine model, emphasising the number of votes influenced by the interests of each industry;

(c) the adjustment-assistance model, taking into consideration the ability of workers to adjust to greater import competition;

(d) the equity-concern model, in which account is taken of the income and skill levels of workers;

(e) the comparative-costs model, taking account of the international competitive strength of each industry;

(f) the international-bargaining model, in which a significant consideration is the bargaining ability and political importance of the
countries from which competing imports are supplied;

(g) the status-quo model, which emphasises the continuity of differential rates of protection; but this begs the question of how
these differential rates arose.

Clearly, while models (a) and (b) relate to the self-interest of participants in the 'political market', models (c) and (d) introduce considerations of equity and model (f) the effect of international pressures.

As the next stage of work along these lines, various attempts have
been made to apply statistical tests in order to determine the relative
force of the various types of explanation. Some results obtained for
various countries of the Community are presented in the Appendix,
where it is concluded that there are certain unavoidable difficulties in
applying statistical tests of the determinants of trade policy in the case
of the Community. A more qualitative approach is therefore taken in
this book.

Distribution of Power and Influence

As alternatives to the ambitious effort in the public choice analysis to
build up a model of the political system on the basis of the preferences of individuals, there are various aggregative models of the
distribution of power and influence at the national level. These draw
attention to the fact that, in countries which are nominally democracies, some people or groups may have more influence on government actions than others. Of particular relevance to this study are the
liberal-democratic, pluralist and corporatist models. One observer
has suggested that:

> Liberal democratic theory rests on the basic assumption that the
> policy preferences of individuals are transmitted to policy makers
> through the electoral system, with the assistance of mediation from
> political parties and interest groups. The political market place is
> held to be analogous to the competitive economy in that the elector
> replaces the consumer as the principal determinant of market
> behaviour.[10]

This model obviously links up with the public choice and political
market approach.

The pluralist view of society, on the other hand, 'suggests that power is dispersed between many groups in society, and in consequence societal decisions are the result of group conflict in which the role of government is one of arbitration among group interests.'[11]

Finally, corporatism is said to denote a system in which the government accords privileged status to consultation with a certain number of representative organisations (representing, for example, industrial managements and trade unions). These organisations then help in the implementation of agreed policies in return for their privileged status.[12]

It may be useful to consider to what extent Germany corresponds with the corporatist model, or the United Kingdom with the pluralist model and whether this illuminates the process of policy formation in these countries and hence in the Community (see Chapters 6 and 8).

Influences on the Decision-makers

In considering the locus of power and influence and the ways in which decisions are made, the relationship between ministers and officials, and between Commissioners and officials in the Commission, is obviously important.

The literature is strewn with references to 'high' and 'low' politics. There is frequently the implication that matters of 'high politics' (defence, for example) are of vital national interest and engage the attention of ministers, while other matters of 'low politics' are of lesser national interest and hence are left to the discretion of officials. This raises the question whether there is in fact any such relationship between the nature of issues and the levels at which they are handled.

Policy makers may see themselves as clear-sighted and rational. The sociological and political science literature emphasises the importance of the 'conceptual spectacles' through which they view the world. These conceptual spectacles affect not only value judgements, but views on relations of cause and effect and, more generally, the selection of the elements of a given situation which are considered relevant. They result from various forms of conditioning – upbringing, formal education, reading and the media, personal and professional experience.

The literature further emphasises the ways in which parts of the government structure – notably ministries, and even individual divisions and sections within ministries – develop their own ethos, to which individuals are brought to conform by processes of conditioning and systems of rewards and penalties. Thus a trade ministry, or parts of a ministry, may have a strong liberal trade orientation, or may be imbued by mercantilist ideas. Sections in an industry ministry follow the affairs of a particular industry and may see the prosperity of the industry as synonymous with the well-being of society. Thus individuals in a national (or international) administration work not only within a system of checks and balances (which, from the point of view of the individual, translates itself into a structure of rewards and penalties) but are also subject to more subtle forms of conditioning.

This chapter has noted four major interpretations of policy-making at Community level – intergovernmental politics, neo-functionalism, transationalism, élite networks. In later chapters these interpretations will be examined further to see which explanatory models are more apposite and also to consider whether decision-making is best explained by a combination of two or more of these models. The nature of the decision-making process at Community level will be further considered in Chapter 9 in the light of the various case studies.

It has been seen that the various models of policy-making at Community level imply views of the extent to which national governments form firm preferences in matters of trade policy and seek to control or influence decisions at Community level. In Chapters 6 to 8, the extent to which the governments of three of the major countries in the Community – Germany, France and the United Kingdom – form deliberate and coordinated views on matters of Community trade policy will be considered together with the influences and considerations which shape the nature of these views.

Of course, views on trade policy have not been formed in a vacuum, but against the background of the prevailing economic circumstances. In the next chapter the economic conditions of the 1970s and 1980s are reviewed and the problems confronting European governments are appraised.

5 Economic Background to Community Trade Policy

Decision-making in matters of trade policy in the 1970s and 1980s has to be seen against the background of the economic developments of the period. Governments were faced with problems of increasing unemployment, inflation, adaptation to the two rounds of major increases in the price of oil, and the need for economic adjustment and restructuring in response to technological developments and changing patterns of international competition. This complex of economic developments and problems is reviewed in the main part of this chapter. The major international trade negotiations of the period are recalled in the final section.

UNEMPLOYMENT

The economic malaise in the Community is shown particularly clearly and directly by the sharp rises in unemployment rates. In the earlier post-war years, it had been generally assumed that the judicious use of macro-economic policy could hold unemployment in advanced, industrial economies down to 'frictional' rates of not more than, say, 3 per cent of the labour force (although in Italy the unemployment rate was around 5 per cent throughout the 1960s).

Figure 5.1 shows the evolution of unemployment rates in the four largest countries of the ten-country Community. Between 1973 or 1974 and 1977, the general experience was of sharp rises of unemployment. After temporary falls in Germany and the United Kingdom (but not in France or Italy), unemployment rates then rose rapidly again, reaching peaks for Germany and the United Kingdom in 1983, for France in 1987 and for Italy in 1988. Unemployment rates were lowest throughout the two decades in Germany, highest in Italy until 1981, when it was overtaken by the United Kingdom. In 1988 to 1990 the order was Italy (highest), France, United Kingdom, and Germany (lowest).

Of course, national average unemployment rates, though themselves high in the 1980s, greatly understate the rates experienced in

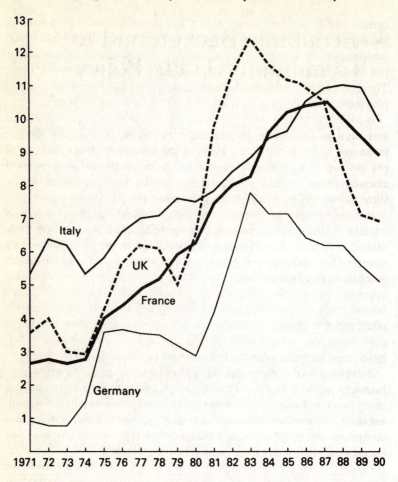

Figure 5.1 Standardised unemployment rates, 1971–90 (per cent of total labour force).

Note: Based on ILO/OECD guidelines. Averages of quarterly or monthly figures.

Source: OECD, *Economic Outlook* (Paris, December 1991).

certain areas, notably those which had been highly dependent on industries hit by stagnant demand and increases in international competition. In some places, Lorraine in France, for example, large job losses or the prospect of job losses have provoked major riots. There has been widespread concern over high levels of youth unemployment and over the increase of long-term unemployment.

In all Community countries, rising unemployment in the mid-1970s was seen as politically dangerous to government and gave rise to pressures to 'do something'. There were widespread fears that workers displaced in declining industries would not find employment elsewhere and it is not surprising that there were calls to bolster up these industries by subsidies or protection.

Increasing unemployment nevertheless provoked more political anxiety in the second half of the 1970s when it was a new phenomenon (Figure 5.1) in post-war terms than in the mid-1980s, even though it had then climbed to considerably higher levels. Much of this acceptance is attributable, no doubt, to social security benefits and to opportunities in the 'informal economy'. Where there have been serious riots, there have been causes other than unemployment – often racial tensions – so that it has been possible for governments to play down the contribution of unemployment, and civil disorders have been sporadic rather than cumulative.

Nevertheless, there was continued anxiety in the 1980s about 'the future of work' and 'de-industrialisation' (exacerbated by the adjustment problems discussed below). This provided fertile soil for interventionist arguments – including at the extreme the argument that competition from countries with radically different economic and social systems is inherently immiserising and protection is therefore necessary.[1] Arguments, however well founded, that subsidies and protection at best shuffle round unemployment from one part of the economy to another, could appear to policy-makers as 'theoretical' in the dismissive sense of the word.

As time went by, it became increasingly apparent that the causes of the malaise – of which intractable mass unemployment was the most obvious symptom – were complex. Views on desirable policies were inevitably influenced by the relative emphasis placed on, and the interpretation given to, the various causative elements. Two of these causative elements are (i) macro-economic management and (ii) the need for major changes in economic structure. These will now be reviewed in turn.

MACRO-ECONOMIC PROBLEMS AND RESPONSES

At the macro-economic level, it is necessary to go back to the widespread boom at the beginning of the 1970s in the countries belonging to the Organisation for Economic Cooperation and Development (OECD). This encouraged inflation, both by stimulating increased wage demands and by leading to a more-than-doubling, between 1971 and 1974, of the average price of primary commodities (excluding oil, gold and precious stones). The commodity price boom was reinforced by the purchase of commodities as a hedge against inflation and against exchange rate movements. The immediate occasion for the major oil price rises of 1973–4 was the war between Israel and Egypt in October 1973; but representatives of the oil-producing countries belonging to the Organisation of Petroleum Exporting Countries (OPEC) had already begun a series of meetings to discuss oil prices earlier in the year, spurred on by the dramatic rises in other primary commodity prices. In the words of one economist:

> It was not events but ideas that propelled us towards the increasing inflation rate. The upward drift in inflation was the result of a fundamental set of beliefs about the economy and macroeconomic policy that were shared by economists and policy officials.[2]

In reaction to increased unemployment combined with rapid inflation ('stagflation'), theories of macro-economic management widely held in the post-war years were increasingly called into doubt during the decade of the 1970s. Governments had to adjust to new theories of economic policy.

Differences in inflation rates in the major trading countries, coupled with increased international capital movements, also led to the breakdown of the Bretton Woods system of fixed, if adjustable, exchange rates. This in turn somewhat relaxed the pressure to pursue disinflationary policies in the countries with the highest rates of inflation.

In August 1971, President Nixon announced that the United States Treasury would suspend purchases and sales of gold (at a fixed dollar price). A 10 per cent surcharge was imposed on all dutiable imports. The attempt to establish a new set of fixed exchange rates was made by the Smithsonian Agreement of December 1971;[3] but this rapidly broke down under the strains of high and differing inflation rates. The United Kingdom went over to a floating exchange rate in June 1972 and with the spread of floating exchange rates, the degree of discipline imposed by an essentially fixed-rate system was relaxed.[4]

First Oil Price Shock

After the dramatic increases in the price of oil in 1973 and 1974, the governments of the OECD countries found themselves in a macroeconomic quandary. On the one hand, huge savings by Saudi Arabia and the other 'low absorber' OPEC countries appeared to withdraw purchasing power from the rest of the world and to threaten a recession in economic activity. On the other hand, the prime need was acknowledged to be to bring down inflation. At the Ministerial Council meeting of the OECD in May 1974, the ministers agreed that:

> They will seek to maintain economic activity at satisfactory levels and avoid policies that would transfer employment problems from one country to another. But Ministers agreed that great care is at present needed to avoid the emergence of excess demand in the OECD area, and that fiscal and monetary policies have to be shaped to this end.[5]

As part of the avoidance of beggar-my-neighbour policies, the Ministers declared their determination for a period of one year,

> . . . to avoid having recourse to unilateral measures, of either a general or a specific nature, to restrict imports or having recourse to similar measures on the other current account transactions, which would be contrary to the objectives of the present Declaration.[6]

This Trade Pledge was then renewed, year by year, in the communiqués of subsequent Ministerial Council meetings.

In the mid-1970s, the United Kingdom experienced large (if progressively declining) deficits on current account and rising inflation rates, peaking in the second half of 1975 at not far short of 30 per cent (half-year on half-year at an annual rate). In 1975 the Labour Government – having been returned in 1974 with an increased majority – introduced a contractionary budget and a tighter monetary policy. Nevertheless, in 1976 the government was obliged to secure a standby credit from the International Monetary Fund (IMF) and to impose further restrictive measures under IMF conditionality. An alternative policy based on the control of imports, advocated by the 'New Cambridge' school of economists and espoused by the left wing of the Labour Party, was rejected largely on the grounds that it would provoke damaging retaliation, notably by the United States, and be inconsistent with British membership of the Community (an attraction to some).

France also had problems of inflation in the mid-1970s. Following a stabilisation programme in 1974, there was an actual decline of gross national product in the first half of 1975. The Government then took expansionary fiscal measures and there was a gradual relaxation of monetary policy. This resulted in a deficit on the current account of the balance of payments and in August 1976, President Giscard d'Estaing appointed Raymond Barre as Prime Minister and Minister of Finance, to carry out a firm deflationary policy.

The macro-economic situation was markedly different in Germany, though here too, given the ingrained horror of inflation, there was anxiety about price rises, which reached about 7 per cent, year on year, in both 1974 and 1975. Demand remained persistently weak, however, leading to stimulatory monetary and fiscal policies.

Second Oil Price Shock

Economies and governments had barely had time to adjust to the consequences of the first oil price shock when the outbreak of war between Iraq and Iran at the end of 1978 led to the second series of increases in the price of oil.

The conventional wisdom on this occasion was summarised by a Communiqué of the OECD Ministerial Council in June 1980:

At their meeting a year ago Ministers agreed that the right response to the inflationary impact of higher oil prices was non-accommodating monetary policies and tight fiscal policies, coupled with important efforts to gain acceptance for the fact that the rise in oil prices reduces, for all social groups, the scope for higher real incomes.

Maintenance of economic growth and improvement in the employment situation was to be sought in 'supply-oriented policies'.[7]

Deflationary policies were pursued particularly vigorously in the

United Kingdom under the premiership of Margaret Thatcher after the election in 1979, but the inflation rate continued to rise partly because of the policy of switching from direct to indirect taxation (thus pushing up retail prices and wage claims). Under the combined influence of deflationary policies and the contribution to the balance of payments of North Sea oil, the sterling exchange rate greatly appreciated, creating major difficulties for manufacturers, both in export markets and at home in competition with imports. Economic activity fell by roughly 7 per cent between the second half of 1979 and the second half of 1981, while the unemployment rate rose rapidly, from nearly 6.5 per cent in 1980 to nearly 12.5 per cent in 1983.

In France, the Socialist government, newly elected in 1981, tried to stimulate economic activity whilst attempting to curb inflation through price control. This led to a deteriorating position on the current account of the balance of payments and the policy was changed to one of 'rigour' and 'increased rigour' in 1982 and 1983. The rate of growth of economic activity slowed and unemployment increased, although at a slower rate than in the United Kingdom.

In Germany, after many years of strong positive balances, the current account went into deficit following the oil price increases and recession in the world economy, in the three years from 1979 to 1981. There were declines in economic activity in the second half of 1980 and in 1982. Nevertheless, the government continued to follow conservative fiscal and monetary policies, resisting calls to act as a 'locomotive' of economic growth. The increase in unemployment, as a percentage of the labour force, between 1973 and 1983 was greater in Germany than in France or Italy (despite the safety valve provided by departure of 'guest workers'), although the level of unemployment was lower throughout.

ECONOMIC RESTRUCTURING

In addition to the macro-economic problems of the 1970s and 1980s, the countries of the Community have been subject to major economic restructuring resulting from changes in the patterns of demand, technological developments and changing conditions in international competition.

A broad outline of this process of restructuring, in terms of the pattern of employment between 1970 and 1987 in Germany, France, the United Kingdom and Italy, is shown in Tables 5.1 (numbers

Table 5.1 Annual average changes of employment and unemployment ('000)

	1970–74	1974–77	1977–80	1980–83	1983–87
Germany					
Employment in: Agriculture	– 105	– 84	– 51	– 15	– 16
Industry	– 186	– 327	+ 64	– 339	– 10
Services	+ 265	+ 72	+ 246	+ 22	+ 186
Total employment	– 26	– 339	+ 260	– 332	+ 160
Registered unemployment	+ 114	+ 143	– 44	+ 455	– 7
Total working population	+ 83	– 190	+ 213	+ 124	+ 153
France					
Employment in: Agriculture	– 157	– 77	– 53	– 59	– 47
Industry	+ 47	– 116	– 97	– 171	– 170
Services	+ 260	+ 229	+ 192	+ 176	+ 164
Total employment	+ 150	+ 35	+ 43	– 54	– 53
Registered unemployment	+ 59	+ 191	+ 126	+ 206	+ 139
Total working population	+ 176	+ 209	+ 153	+ 115	+ 90

United Kingdom

Employment in: Agriculture	−25	−4	−6	−11	−8
Industry	−113	−252	−86	−546	−85
Services	+233	+163	+252	−15	+437
Total employment	+95	−92	+160	−572	+345
Registered unemployment	+3	+264	+77	+485	−69[a]
Total working population	+88	+184	+211	−82	+325

Italy

Employment in: Agriculture	−117	−90	−77	−124	−89
Industry	+12	+4	+27	−116	−159
Services	+164	+227	+229	+257	+321
Total employment	+60	+141	+179	+17	+73
Registered unemployment	+27	+49	+145	+298	n.a.
Total working population	+60	+256	+224	+208	+240[a]

a. 1984–87

Source: Eurostat, *Employment and Unemployment* yearbooks (Luxembourg: Statistical Office of the European Communities, 1985, 1988 and 1989).

General notes: see p. 61.

Table 5.2 Annual average changes of employment and unemployment (per cent per annum, compound)

	1970–74	1974–77	1977–80	1980–83	1983–87
Germany					
Employment in: Agriculture	−5.0	−4.8	−3.3	−1.1	−1.2
Industry	−1.5	−2.8	+0.6	−3.1	−0.1
Services	+2.2	+0.6	+1.9	+0.1	+1.3
Total employment	−0.1	−1.3	+1.0	−1.3	+0.6
Registered unemployment	+42.0	+19.6	−4.4	+36.0	−0.3
Total working population	+0.3	−0.7	+0.8	+0.4	+0.5
France					
Employment in: Agriculture	−6.1	−3.7	−2.7	−3.3	−2.9
Industry	+0.6	−1.4	−1.2	−2.3	−2.5
Services	+2.5	+2.0	+1.6	+1.4	+1.2
Total employment	+0.7	+0.2	+0.2	−0.2	−0.2
Registered unemployment	+17.4	+29.1	+10.6	+12.5	+6.1
Total working population	+0.8	+0.9	+0.7	+0.5	+0.4
United Kingdom					
Employment in: Agriculture	−3.3	−0.6	−0.9	−1.7	−1.2
Industry	−1.0	−2.5	−0.9	−6.2	−1.1
Services	+1.7	+1.2	+1.7	−0.1	+2.8
Total employment	+0.4	−0.4	+0.6	−2.3	+1.4
Registered unemployment	+0.4	+33.8	+5.3	+24.2	−2.2[a]
Total working population	+0.3	+0.7	+0.8	−0.3	+1.2
Italy					
Employment in: Agriculture	−3.2	−2.7	−2.5	−4.5	−3.7
Industry	+0.2	+0.1	+0.4	−1.5	−2.2
Services	+1.9	+2.5	+2.3	+2.4	+2.8

Total employment	+0.3	+0.7	+0.9	+0.1	+0.3
Registered unemployment	+2.9	+4.7	+11.3	+16.1	n.a.
Total working population	+0.3	+1.2	+1.0	+0.9	+1.0[a]

a. 1984–87.

Source: As for Table 5.2.

Notes to Tables 5.1 and 5.2

Two caveats apply to the interpretation of the data in these two tables.

First, in the source material, 'total working population' is defined as comprising all persons in employment and the unemployed. The figures for employment in agriculture, industry and services, adding up to 'total employment', '. . . comprise all persons bound to an enterprise by an employment contract'. This would appear to exclude the self-employed and proprietors of private businesses. Hence it would appear that the figures for total working population should be uniformly greater than total employment plus registered unemployed. This is the case for some of the countries in some years; but in other years the total working population is shown as *less* than the sum of total unemployment and the registered unemployed. Because of the discrepancies in either direction, figures in Table 5.1 for changes in total employment and registered unemployment usually do not add up to the changes in total working population. Unfortunately, clarification of the apparent discrepancies has not been forthcoming from the Community's statistical office.

Second, in order to show changes in these two tables over the periods 1970–4 and 1974–7, it has been necessary to use unrevised annual data from the 1985 yearbook, since the revised figures in the later editions are shown only for 1970, with annual data only from 1975 onwards. Estimates for the chosen cyclical periods therefore chain together unrevised data for 1970–4 and 1974–5 with revised data for 1975 onwards.

The most significant discrepancies are in the data for France:

	France, annual average changes, 1970–75			
	('000)		(per cent, compound)	
	Revised	Unrevised	Revised	Unrevised
Employment in: Agriculture	–119	–143	–4.8	–5.7
Industry	+16	–12	+0.2	–0.1
Services	+212	+232	+2.0	+2.2
Total employment	+110	+77	+0.5	+0.4
Total working population	+184	+155	+0.8	+0.7

For the United Kingdom, the 1989 yearbook, which gives year-by-year figures only from 1980 onwards, shows comparatively minor revisions by comparison with the 1988 yearbook.

The latest yearbook gives figures for registered unemployment annually from 1970 onwards, but there are breaks in the series for the United Kingdom between 1983 and 1984, and for Italy between 1985 and 1986.

Despite these problems, the two tables may be taken as giving a general impression of the evolution of employment and unemployment in the four countries.

involved) and 5.2 (annual percentage changes). The periods are chosen to reflect cyclical variations in industrial employment, total employment and unemployment, subject to the qualification that the turning points were not identical in the four countries.

General characteristics of the situation it all four countries were:

(1) Gradual increase of the working population (defined in principle as all persons in employment plus the unemployed; but see notes to Tables 5.1 and 5.2). This was slowest over the period as a whole in Germany, in part because of departure of 'guest workers' when the employment situation was unfavourable.

(2) Progressive decline of the number of employees in agriculture, largest in absolute and percentage terms in France and Italy, where the initial percentages of the working population in agriculture were relatively high, least in the United Kingdom, where employment in agriculture was already small in 1970.

(3) Progressive increase of employment in services, ranging from an average rate of 1.3 per cent per annum over the whole period in Germany to 2.4 per cent in Italy.

(4) Declines in industrial employment, though with fairly marked cyclical fluctuations.

(5) Consequent very gradual growth of total employment (and even a decrease in Germany over the period as a whole), so that the general picture is of failure of employment to keep up with increases in working population.

In view of the upsurge of protectionist sentiment in 1977, particular interest attaches to developments in the period of generally increasing unemployment between 1974 and 1977. During this period, the displacement of labour from agriculture and industry combined amounted to 4.5 per cent of the total initial working population in Germany (where the unemployment rate rose sharply between 1973 and 1975, even if it still remained the lowest for the four countries). The displacement from agriculture and industry amounted to 3.0 per cent of the total working population in the United Kingdom; to 2.6 per cent in France; and to 1.2 per cent in Italy (where the unemployment rate was nevertheless the highest, and rising).

This overall picture does not bring out the displacement of labour from particular industries, with effects on the economy of particular areas and on demands for particular types of labour. Table 5.3 shows annual average percentage changes in employment in five industries which, in the four countries, generally experienced greater decreases of employment than did industry as a whole. The five industry groups are defined as:

— production and preliminary processing of metals (employment figures for steel being shown as a sub-item);
— manufacture of motor vehicles and of vehicle parts and accessories;
— electrical engineering (which excludes manufacture of office machinery and of data processing machinery);
— textile industry;
— footwear and clothing industry.

(Separate figures are not available for other crisis industries such as shipbuilding.)

Of these industries, there were increases of employment over the whole period from 1974 to the second half of the 1980s only for manufacture of motor vehicles and parts in Germany and for the clothing industry in Italy. Otherwise, the general picture for the five industry groups is of relatively rapid reduction of employment. Leaving aside the sub-item of steel, of 75 cells in Table 5.3 (countries/periods/industries) just over half show annual rates of decrease of employment of 3 per cent or more, and of these 16 (21 per cent of the total) show rates of decrease of 5 per cent or more. These five industry groups together accounted for about a quarter of total industrial employment in each of the four countries, but contributed a considerably larger share of the loss of industrial employment: in both of the relatively depressed periods 1974–7 and 1980–3, in both Germany and the United Kingdom (and in France in 1980–3), the five industry groups combined accounted for around one-third of the reduction in industrial employment. (The proportion for France in the period 1974–7 is unavailable because of discontinuities in the figures.) For Italy, the picture is somewhat different. In 1974–7, reductions of employment in motor vehicles and parts, electrical engineering and textiles were largely offset by increases in production and preliminary processing of metals and footwear and clothing, and for industry as a whole there was a slight increase in total employment. On the other hand, in the period 1980–3 the five industry groups accounted for over 40 per cent of the reduction of industrial employment. (The absolute figures for the five industry groups and for total industrial employment are shown in Table 5.4).

Against this background of reductions in industrial employment and increases of unemployment, already in the second half of the

Table 5.3 Changes of employment in selected industrial sectors
(per cent per annum, compound)

	1974–77	1977–80	1980–83	1983–87
Germany				
Metals	− 3.2	− 2.4	− 4.7	− 3.3
(of which: iron and steel)	(− 2.4)	(− 2.1)	(− 5.6)	(− 5.0)
Motor vehicles	− 0.8	+ 3.8	− 1.7	+ 2.7
Electrical and electronic	− 4.0	+ 0.4	− 3.3	+ 2.8
Textiles	− 5.5	− 2.3	− 7.2	− 1.2
Footwear and clothing	− 3.3	− 1.2	− 6.6	− 2.6
Total industry	− 2.8	+ 0.6	− 3.1	− 0.1
France				
Metals	n.a.	− 6.9	− 4.8	− 4.7[a]
(of which: iron and steel)	(− 1.3)	(− 8.7)	(− 6.6)	(− 8.1)[a]
Motor vehicles	n.a.	− 0.6	− 3.5	− 5.1[a]
Electrical and electronic	n.a.	− 1.0	− 0.6	− 1.6[a]
Textiles	n.a.	− 3.0	− 4.5	− 4.0[a]
Footwear and clothing	n.a.	− 2.5	− 4.7	− 4.3[a]
Total industry	− 1.4	− 1.2	− 2.3	− 2.8[a]

United Kingdom

Metals	−1.4	−3.5[b]	−15.4	−6.7
(of which: iron and steel)	(−2.1)	(−9.5)	(−20.4)	(−5.0)
Motor vehicles	−2.3	−0.5[b]	−12.5	−5.5
Electrical and electronic	−3.6	−0.3[b]	−6.5	−2.5
Textiles	−4.4	−6.2[b]	−10.8	−1.9
Footwear and clothing	−3.3	−3.1[b]	−8.6	+0.3
Total industry	−2.5	−0.9	−6.2	−1.1

Italy

Metals	+2.8	+0.1	−2.5	−16.2[c]
(of which: iron and steel)	(+1.3)	(+1.1)	(−3.5)	(−11.3)[c]
Motor vehicles	−3.1	+4.1	−8.7	+4.8[c]
Electrical and electronic	+1.4	−0.8	−2.6	−4.7[c]
Textiles	−3.7	−1.0	−0.9	−6.0[c]
Footwear and clothing	+4.1	−0.8	−1.5	+3.8[c]
Total industry	+0.1	+0.4	−1.5	−3.2[c]

a. 1983–86
b. 1977–78 and 1979–80
c. 1983–85

Table 5.4 Annual average changes of employment in selected industrial sectors ('000)

	1974–77	1977–80	1980–83	1983–87
Germany				
Metals	−14.9	−10.1	−17.5	−10.8
(of which: iron and steel)	(−5.5)	(−4.4)	(−10.7)	(−7.9)
Motor vehicles	−4.9	+24.2	+11.6	+18.5
Electrical and electronic	−44.3	+4.5	−33.1	+28.0
Textiles	−22.1	−7.9	−22.4	−3.2
Footwear and clothing	−13.1	−4.5	−22.1	−7.2
Total of above	−99.3	+6.2	−106.7	+25.3
Total industry	−327	+64	−339	−10
France				
Metals	n.a.	−18.8	−10.7	−9.0[a]
(of which: iron and steel)	(−2.1)	(−12.0)	(−7.0)	(−6.9)[a]
Motor vehicles	n.a.	−2.9	−16.1	−20.7[a]
Electrical and electronic	n.a.	−5.3	−2.8	−7.7[a]
Textiles	n.a.	−9.5	−12.7	−9.8[a]
Footwear and clothing	n.a.	−9.0	−15.1	−12.1[a]
Total of above	n.a.	−45.5	−57.4	−59.3[a]
Total industry	−116	−97	−171	−194

United Kingdom

Metals	−6.5	−15.4[b]	−47.7	−13.4
(of which: iron and steel)	(−3.9)	(−15.5)	(−22.0)	(−3.1)
Motor vehicles	−11.2	−2.3[b]	−49.4	−15.3
Electrical and electronic	−27.1	−2.4[b]	−45.7	−14.8
Textiles	−22.3	−27.7[b]	−34.4	−4.8
Footwear and clothing	−15.3	−13.4[b]	−31.1	+0.8
Total of above	−82.4	−61.2	−208.3	−47.5
Total industry	−252	−86	−546	−85

Italy

Metals	+7.5	+0.3	−7.0	−38.8[c]
(of which: iron and steel)	(+1.2)	(+1.1)	(−3.4)	(−9.6)[c]
Motor vehicles	−7.7	+9.9	−20.8	−9.8[c]
Electrical and electronic	−5.5	−3.2	−9.8	−16.3[c]
Textiles	−19.6	−4.9	−4.2	−27.0[c]
Footwear and clothing	+21.2	−4.4	−8.3	+20.4[c]
Total of above	−4.1	−2.3	−50.1	−71.5[c]
Total industry	+4	+27	−116	−228[c]

a. 1983–86
b. 1977–78 and 1979–80
c. 1983–85

1970s there was a growing concern with the 'adjustment problem', attention focusing in particular on the effects of increased competition from Japan and the newly-industrialising countries of south-east Asia.[8]

INTERNATIONAL DISCUSSIONS ON TRADE POLICY

There is a two-way connection between macro- and micro-economic problems on the one hand and trade policies on the other. Protective measures, including voluntary restraint agreements with exporting countries, have been seen as a way of reducing immediate economic and social problems at home. Conversely, there are strong arguments that such protectionist measures have exacerbated domestic problems by imposing costs on other parts of the economies and by reducing the incentives to make necessary adjustments. Thus in the case of Germany it is commonly argued that governments have been able to resist protectionist pressures from the manufacturing sector because of a successful blend of macro- and micro-economic policies – that Germany achieved a virtuous spiral in a way that France and the United Kingdom, for example, did not.

Tokyo Round Negotiations

One effect of the first oil price shock was to delay progress in the Tokyo Round of trade negotiations in the GATT. The preceding Kennedy Round had ended in 1967. Then, for a period of five years, there was no agreement to embark on a new round. In March 1972, however, the GATT Council took a decision in principle on the launching of a new round the following year. The Tokyo Declaration, agreed by ministers in September 1973, states that:

> The negotiations shall aim to: – achieve the expansion and ever-growing liberalisation of world trade and improvement in the standard of living and welfare of the people of the world, objectives which can be achieved, inter alia, through the progressive dismantling of obstacles to trade and the improvement of the international framework for the conduct of world trade.[9]

Governments then became enmeshed in the problems arising from accelerating inflation and the first oil price shock; the Tokyo Round negotiations dragged on without significant progress.

Indeed, in 1977 the GATT Secretariat stated that 'The spread of protectionist pressures . . . has reached a point at which the continued existence of an international order based on agreed and observed rules may be said to be open to question'. While it was not difficult to identify the sources of the pressure for protection, governments were acting in contradiction to their stated policy objectives.[10]

By 1977, even the annual renewal of the OECD Trade Pledge ran into various doubts and hesitations. *Agence Europe* suggested that, whereas the United States Administration wished to strengthen the provisions, the British authorities considered that the commitments involved were 'unbalanced'.[11] The French government, too, was looking in other directions. At the London Economic Summit in April 1977, President Giscard d'Estaing advocated regulation of trade under the slogan of 'organised liberalism'. This failed to find favour. The Summit Declaration stated:

> We reject protectionism: it would foster unemployment, increase inflation and undermine the welfare of our peoples. We will give a new impetus to the Tokyo Round . . .

On the other hand, an Appendix to the Declaration added:

> Such progress should not remove the right of individual countries under existing international agreements to avoid significant market disruption.

This was no doubt a reference, in part at least, to the desire in the Community to tighten up protection under the MFA. In May 1977, the Community reached agreement to support a further extension for one year of the OECD Trade Pledge.

Despite these cross-currents, the Tokyo Round negotiations picked up momentum in 1977 and were completed in 1979. A further round of tariff cuts was agreed. In addition there were certain agreements relating to quantitative restrictions to trade, such as the Agreement on Technical Barriers to Trade and the Agreement on Government Procurement. On one important question – strengthening or modification of the rules governing safeguard protection – no agreement could be reached. Any attempt at international discipline on safeguard protection has in any case been largely circumvented by resort to voluntary restraint agreements – though there have been signs that the Community has become disillusioned with the effects of such agreements and considers the alternative of increases in tariffs. The text of a code on subsidies and countervailing duties was agreed, but this papered over continuing disagreements between the Community and the United States concerning the permissibility of subsidies for reasons of domestic policy – disagreements which have continued to give rise to disputes.

Positive Adjustment Policies

Another strand in international discussions bearing on trade policy was the work programme in the OECD on 'positive adjustment policies', launched in 1979. (The countries of the Community are individually members of the OECD.)

This work programme was concerned largely with questions of internal economic management. The Communiqué adopted at the July 1979 Ministerial Council stated:

> Positive adjustment should rely as far as possible on market forces to encourage mobility of labour and capital to their most productive uses. Measures to help sectors or firms in difficulty should be temporary and integrally linked to the implementation of plans to phase out obsolete capacity and re-establish financially viable entities.[12]

The work also had more direct implications for trade policy. In an annex to its Communiqué of May 1982, the OECD Ministerial Council 'particularly underline that the maintenance of an open multilateral trading system is crucial to achieving the objectives of positive adjustment'.[13] An earlier Communiqué, of June 1978, had noted that domestic measures to cushion the impact of economic adjustment 'may have much the same effect as protection at the frontier in enabling inefficient producers to compete with foreign suppliers and in delaying necessary structural adjustments. They may both create a vested interest in protection in the country concerned, and provoke protectionist reactions in other countries'.[14]

Approach to the Uruguay Round

As well as the second set of oil price increases and the subsequent collapse of the price of oil, the other major economic developments influencing thinking on trade policy in the Community in recent years have been outside the Community itself.

The first has been the strengthening of protectionist policies in the United States, exacerbated by a persistently large negative trade balance, itself associated with the continuing Federal budget deficit and the continued willingness of the outside world to lend to, and invest in, the United States. Not only has the Community been involved in a series of defensive actions against protectionism in the United States but it has also been constrained in its own policies by the need to consider potential reactions in that country.

The second has been the return of Japan to large and persistent current account surpluses, which have been widely seen as reducing the opportunities open to Community producers.

In the early 1980s, governments felt increasing alarm at the risks of spreading protectionism. In the declaration agreed at the GATT ministerial meeting of November 1982, the participants 'reaffirm[ed] their commitment to abide by their GATT obligations and to support and improve the GATT trading system . . .'[15] The OECD Ministerial Council of May 1983 went further, agreeing to the statement:

> that the economic recovery, as it proceeds, provides favourable conditions which Member Countries should use, individually and collectively, to reverse protectionist trends and to relax or dismantle progressively trade restrictions and trade distorting domestic measures, particularly those introduced over the recent period of poor growth performance.'[16]

A year later the OECD Ministerial Council agreed that the Final tariff cuts scheduled in the Tokyo Round should be advanced by a year, subject to completion of the necessary procedures.[17] It was during this period that the phrase 'standstill and rollback' of protective measures gained currency. Commission officials felt that the Community would have greater difficulty in rolling back quantitative restrictions, including voluntary restraint agreements.

Also in the early 1980s, voices in the United States began informally canvassing the idea of strengthened trade rules among countries which would agree – a 'Super-GATT' or 'GATT of the like-minded'. These ideas failed to find favour, the Community taking the view that in future, developing countries should be more rather than less involved in the GATT. Both the United States and Japan then began to press for the launching of a new round of trade negotiations. In the Community the Council agreed, in March 1985, that: 'Subject to the establishment of an adequate prior international consensus on objectives, participation and timing, the Community declares its readiness to participate in the launching of a new round.' Under pressure, in particular from the French Government, the declaration stated: 'The Council is determined that the fundamental objectives and mechanisms, both internal and external, of the Common Agricultural Policy shall not be placed in question.' On the other hand (as seen in Chapter 2) the French were beaten back in their insistence that action to stabilise exchange rates should be a precondition for further negotiations on trade.

At the Economic Summit in Bonn in May 1985, the German Chancellor and the Prime Minister of the United Kingdom were prepared to accept a proposed date for the opening of a new round, but President Mitterrand refused, arguing that the negotiations had not yet been sufficiently prepared.

Two issues in particular continued to give rise to doubts on the successful launching of a new round: (i) the treatment of trade in agricultural products, and (ii) the resistance of a number of major developing countries to negotiations on the rules to govern trade in services. The Uruguay Round of multilateral trade negotiations was nevertheless formally launched at a meeting of trade ministers in Punta del Este in September 1986. The preparation of negotiating positions for the round then became a major preoccupation of Community trade policy.

This chapter has sketched the background against which decisions in the Community on trade policy were made in the 1970s and 1980s – the major economic developments and problems of the period and the climate of international discussions bearing on trade policy. The next three chapters will consider the attitudes, pressures and institutional arrangements shaping positions on trade policy in three of the largest countries of the Community, Germany, France and the United Kingdom.

6 Making Trade Policy in Germany[1]

Two central questions were posed at the outset of this study; how have decisions on trade policy been made in the European Community and what influences have shaped these decisions. It has been seen that these questions raise issues about the form and substance of policy making at the national level.

On the question of how decisions are made, the interpretation of policy-making in the Community as a matter of inter-governmental negotiation implies that the member governments take effective steps to ensure that the views which carry most weight are 'national' views as expressed by representatives of the governments. This in turn raises the question of how positions on policy are formed within the various national administrations, and how effective is the control over those who represent the various governments at Community level. Alternative views suggest either that positions on policy advanced by national ministers or officials in the Council or its subordinate bodies are not effectively coordinated within the various administrations or that governments stand aside while particular interests, either private or from within the government machine, exercise effective pressure on the making of Community policies. These questions concerning the behaviour of governments can be best answered by an examination of policy-making in some of the larger countries of the Community.

It will be assumed at this point as a working hypothesis that views on policy advanced in the names of the various member governments have a substantial influence on policy decisions at Community level. It is then relevant to ask why these views have often differed as between the various countries. What have been the major influences on trade policy within countries?

Accordingly, this chapter and the two following consider in turn the making of trade policy in Germany, France and the United Kingdom. These chapters:

(a) give illustrations of each country's approach in matters of trade policy;

(b) consider the ideas that have influenced policy and how these ideas relate to, or are influenced by, each country's institutional arrangements;

(c) outline the evolution of trade policy in each of the countries over the years since World War II and in particular its relationship to industrial policy;

(d) review in more detail each country's institutional arrangements as they affect the making of trade policy;

(e) examine the political pressures on the policy makers;

(f) discuss the effectiveness of the arrangements for coordination of policy on matters of Community trade policy.

A VOICE FOR LIBERALISM

Successive German governments have argued rather consistently for liberal import policies for manufactured goods within the Community. The German position, as it was then and as it has remained in essentials, was set out in a memorandum sent to the Council of the Community in 1978 by Count Otto von Lambsdorff (German Economics Minister from 1977 to 1984). This reads in part:

> measures to preserve [economic] structures . . . impede techno-logical, economic and social progress, and cause long-term damage to the international competitiveness of the Community, and are thus unsuitable for permanently protecting endangered jobs.
>
> In the event of it proving necessary in very limited exceptions to slow down the process of adjustment to the market on regional or social grounds in view of the slow rate of growth and major employ-ment problems with which we are at present confronted, *temporary arrangements* may be allowed *for a fixed period of time* provided that they act as an inducement to self-help and do not stand in the way of necessary adjustments to changes in market conditions.

The memorandum goes on to state:

> The German Government . . . only agreed to measures regulat-ing imports in the textiles and steel sectors with considerable reservations, in order to avoid the threat of national protection measures and in order to maintain the degree of integration already achieved in the EEC.[2]

A further written statement in favour of liberal trade policies produced for internal consumption, was given to the lower house of the German parliament in June 1984. There was an essential continuity of policy under Count Lambsdorff's successor, Martin Bangemann, who was Economics Minister from 1984 to 1988.

It has to be noted that these statements of liberal economic principles apply more to the industrial sector than to some other parts of the German economy, notably agriculture and trade in services, even within the Community itself. At home, there are various regional subsidies as well as national subsidies or favourable tax treatment for coal-mining, shipbuilding, the railways and postal services, together with special aids for research and development and for small businesses. For shipbuilding, for example, it can be said that the Germans have been able to pose as liberal traders in Brussels because they assist their own industry by indirect means (for example, tax concessions to shipowners and private investors in shipbuilding) rather than by more direct means. Many types of manufacturing are commonly said to receive a considerable degree of protection resulting from the administration, by the industries themselves, of standards with which imported goods must comply. As a result, the industries see no need to press for other forms of protection.

Even when the agricultural sector is left aside, it would be misleading to present Germany as a Simon Pure example of free market principles. Nevertheless, the fact remains that, at any rate up to the early 1990s, German governments have rather consistently opposed protective measures by the Community for manufactured goods. In this their approach has differed markedly from that of French governments and, if in lesser degree, from the attitude of past governments in the United Kingdom. It is thus relevant to enquire into the sources of these differences of approach.

DOMINANT INFLUENCES ON POLICY

In Germany, five elements have combined to support free-market attitudes, particularly in relation to manufacturing.

First, after World War II, there was a conscious decision to adopt a generally free-market approach, underpinned by social welfare provisions – the 'social market' approach – and this was bolstered by the desire to distance the Federal Republic both from the Nazi past and from the East German system. Second, this approach was validated by the 'economic miracle' of the earlier post-war years. Third, despite a change in the dominant party in the Federal governments, from the Social Democratic Party (SDP) in the 1970s to the Christian Democratic Union (CDU) since 1982, the exigencies of coalition forming led since 1972 to the appointment of Federal Economics Ministers drawn from the right wing of the minority Free Democratic Party (FDP), which has favoured liberal trade policies. Fourth, the broader institutional structure, as it relates to manufacturing, has been such as to put upholders of the social market orthodoxy in positions of power and influence. Finally, there has been a tendency in both the administrative and political machines to treat economic issues in a technocratic way.

There are, in fact, different views even among officials of the Economics Ministry on the essential rationale of the German approach to trade policy. Some stress the need to avoid economic distortions and to apply market pressures for necessary economic restructuring, maintaining that emphasis on Germany's high dependence on exports is no more than a convenient selling-point. Others argue that the policy orientation is essentially pragmatic – that a country which has prospered with the help of a successful export performance needs, as a practical matter, to work for an open international trading system and to expose the internal economy to the pressures of external competition: 'If our industries cannot compete in the domestic market, they cannot expect to be able to export.' Obviously, this is essentially a matter of emphasis, since the two approaches overlap and point in the same policy direction.

Another important consideration is the need for a country which has prospered on the basis of flourishing exports to avoid retaliatory protection by trading partners (an argument stressed in the 1978 Memorandum to the Council). In relation to the Community's policy towards Japan, the German governments have also been activated by fears that some of the same objections which are made towards Japanese policies could also be turned against Germany.[3]

DEVELOPMENTS IN TRADE AND INDUSTRIAL POLICY

The principles of the social market economy were advocated, and to a great extent applied, by Ludwig Erhard when he was Minister of Economic Affairs from 1949 to 1963 and Chancellor (Prime Minister) from 1963 to 1966.[4]

In the 1950s and 1960s, nevertheless, several industries, including iron and steel production, non-ferrous metals, cellulose, paper and board, leather and shoes, textiles and clothing, received substantial protection. There were subsidies for shipbuilding, and subsequently for the development of civil aircraft.[5]

By about 1970, the stated policy had become one of 'putting the economy to the test of bearing burdens'.[6] The market should be the driving force for efficient structural change. 'It is only in particular cases that specific and highly targeted aids should be given in order to improve regional or sectoral economic structures.'[7]

With the undervaluation of the Deutschmark until the late 1960s, manufactured exports and manufacturing in general flourished and so industrial restructuring – for example, the running down of the textile industry – proceeded relatively smoothly. The problems of German steel producers were met by cartel arrangements: from 1976 they extended their existing 'rationalisation groupings' to include steel producers in Luxembourg, the Netherlands and Belgium. Close association between the banks and industry has facilitated industrial restructuring within the ambit of the private sector, and hence largely outside the political arena.[8] Finally, as already mentioned, much manufacturing in Germany has enjoyed an informal variety of protection through the administration, by industry associations, of extensive regulations on standards for manufactured goods.

Despite the persistence of free-market principles, especially in the Economics Ministry, the German authorities became increasingly concerned in the 1980s with questions of 'fairness' and reciprocity in international trade. In 1992, the German authorities joined the Italians and French in persuading the Commission to authorise safeguard protection, under the terms of the association agreement with the Czech and Slovak Federal Republic, against certain steel products. The association of the German steel industry was quoted as saying that it hoped that this would send a signal to exporters of other cheap steel products and to other East European countries.[9] This piece of protection might simply show the force of the 'fairness' argument, or it might point to a modification of the established liberal trade approach, under pressure of the economic problems of reunification.

INSTITUTIONAL ARRANGEMENTS

The free-market approach to manufacturing industry in Germany has been bolstered by various features of the institutional arrangements: the strong role of the Economics Ministry; the tendency in the Federal Parliament to treat questions of trade policy as essentially technical matters; and the workings of a corporatist system of consultation on economic issues.

Role of the Economics Ministry

Under the German constitution (Basic Law), although the Federal Chancellor has overall responsibility for government policy, Article 65 lays down that the various ministers are to conduct the business of their departments 'autonomously'.

Within this framework, responsibility for trade policy affecting industrial products lies with the Economics Ministry (*Bundminister-ium für Wirtschaft*). Differences of view between officials dealing with industrial matters and the department responsible for trade policy are largely settled within this Ministry. The officials dealing with external trade tend to conform to the established tradition of liberalism (though with the different interpretations of the underlying rationale noted above). They are supported within the ministry by a strong Economic Policy Department, which has the task of considering the interrelationship of different aspects of economic policy. (It is largely from this department that professional economic advice is brought to bear on the work of the ministry as a whole.) The Economic Policy Department is an ally of the department with responsibility for matters of external trade in fighting off the particular sectoral interests which are transmitted through the sections of the ministry covering the various industries.

Within the German administration, the Economics Ministry is in a strong position in matters of Community trade and industrial policies (always leaving on one side the special question of agriculture). While the German Permanent Representative to the Communities comes from the Foreign Ministry, responsibility for briefing on external trade and industrial matters lies with the Economics Ministry.

There may nevertheless be conflicting pressures from other ministers. Some questions of industrial policy involve the (separate) Technology Ministry. This has a greater tendency to favour intervention and protection, but politically has been relatively weak. Other parts of the Federal Government, too, by no means share the attachment of the Economics Ministry to free-market principles, notably the Ministries of Agriculture, Transport, and Posts and Telecommunications. The Foreign Ministry, for its part, emphasises Community cooperation, and this may bring it into conflict with the liberal economic views of the Economics Ministry.

Role of Parliament

The tendency to treat matters of trade policy largely as technical questions is also present in the parliament (*Bundestag* and *Bundesrat*). Three elements combine to produce this result.

First, the broad principles of a free-market approach for manufacturing have not been in dispute between the major political parties. Whilst the Social Democrats are more responsive to the claims of the unions than the more right wing parties, there is nothing like the opposition between free-market principles and *dirigisme* found, for example, in United Kingdom politics. This is due in part to the dominant influences on policy reviewed above, in part to the competition of the two mass parties, the SDP and the CDU, for the middle ground in German politics. Challenges to the economic policy consensus, notably from the Green Party, which stresses environmental issues, and from the left wing of the Social Democratic Party, have been contained.

Second, many members of the parliament are selected on the basis of expertise. While half the members of the *Bundestag* are directly elected by parliamentary districts, half are elected by proportional representation on the basis of lists of candidates for the various *Länder*. The *Bundesrat* consists essentially of delegations of the governments of the *Länder*. Under this system, many members of the *Bundestag* are government officials from either Federal or *Land* level on leave of absence.

Third, discussion of Community matters in the *Bundestag* and *Bundesrat* takes place largely in committee. 'The volume of legislation inspired by post-war issues, the need for specialisation to master the complex subject matter, and the desire of interested representatives to remove the issues of concern to them to committees which they could dominate, all contributed to this development.'[10] Committees in the *Bundestag* may invite witnesses from relevant interest groups, though these groups will often have submitted their views in written memoranda. Government officials from the ministries involved have access to the committees, as do representatives of the *Bundesrat*. The discussion is typically technical, rather than a matter of conflict between government and opposition parties.[11]

Article 2 of the German Act of Ratification of the Rome Treaties lays down that:

> The Federal Government shall keep the *Bundestag* and the *Bundesrat* continually informed of developments in the Council of the European Economic Community and in the Council of the European Atomic Energy Community.[12] Insofar as a decision of a Council requires the making of a German law or has immediate force of law in the Federal Republic of Germany, notification should be made prior to the Council making its decision.

The Federal Government has adhered to a broad interpretation of the matters on which the Parliament should be kept informed. Nevertheless, in the nature of things, the two houses tend to be brought in at a stage when Community proposals have already begun to take shape.[13] (The *Länder*, however, maintain a permanent observer in Brussels to keep track of developments there, and individual *Länder* have opened their own liaison offices).

Debates in the *Bundestag* on Community matters have been infrequent. There has been occasional use of '*aktuelle Stunde*', hour-long adjournment debates on subjects of current interest. From time to time, Community matters have been made the subject of written questions (*kleine Anfragen*), or written questions leading to a short debate (*grosse Anfragen*). This procedure is slow, however, and members of the *Bundesrat* have made more use of oral questions. These can be raised at short notice and supplementary questions asked. The answers tend to be rather formal; but such questions, often inspired by interest groups, can nevertheless be used as a means of pressure on the government.[14]

Only for certain major issues is it necessary for the Federal Government to obtain the approval of the *Bundestag* and *Bundesrat* for Community decisions. The *Bundestag* and *Bundesrat* do not have the power to make binding decisions on how the Federal Government shall act in the Community Council (a power possessed by the Market Relations Committee in the Danish parliament). Under a sifting procedure introduced in 1978, proposals on Community matters are only discussed in committee if a member specifically requests this within the short time permitted. Proposals on which no deputy expresses an interest are accepted under a list procedure. Interest groups, however, have an incentive to try to ensure that their views shall not be lost by default during the time allowed for parliamentary scrutiny, since this would weaken their bargaining position with the Federal Government.[15]

German-style Corporatism

In Germany, the economic policy of the Federal Government is made in consultation with broad interest groups, notably the Association of Germany Industry (*Bundesverband der Deutschen Industrie* – BDI), and the German Conference of Chambers of Industry and Commerce (*Deutscher Industrie und Handelstag* – DIHT).[16]

Both the BDI and the DIHT have supported the liberal approach to trade policy of the successive Economics Ministers and the Economics Ministry. This illustrates the proposition that broadly-based peak organisations can take a balanced view of the national interest, since within such organisations particular sectional interests tend to cancel out.

The DIHT coordinates the views of over 70 chambers of industry and commerce. These bodies were established by the 1956 Chambers of Commerce and Industry Act. Their responsibilities are laid down by the Federal Government. Membership is compulsory for all incorporated businesses. The duty is placed on local chambers to take a view on behalf of their areas and not of particular industrial interests. Thus it is said that, even in areas with a considerable concentration of textile manufacturing, the chambers take a view which by no means concentrates on the needs of this particular industry. In addition, the headquarters organisation in Bonn uses its links with the local chambers to emphasise the virtues of free-market policies.

While the DIHT reflects regional views, the BDI reflects the views of manufacturing, industry by industry. At the same time, the central organisation is much impressed by the dependence of many of its members – for example, engineering firms – on exports. It subscribes to the free-market approach of the Economics Ministry, while accepting that this may not be to the liking of some of its members. In relation to the Multifibre Arrangement, for example, the Textile Industry Association insists on speaking for itself, arguing that it knows the detail while the BDI does not.

As one manifestation of the corporatist approach, there is consultation with exporting and importing interests and members of the

Bundestag, through the Advisory Council for External Economic Affairs (*Aussenwirtschaftsbeirat*). This is chaired by an official from the trade side of the Economics Ministry, but the Minister regularly attends its meetings, which take place approximately twice a year.

The trade unions in Germany have not been particularly strong as a political force. At the peak level, representation of German unions is highly concentrated in the *Deutsche Gewerkshaftsbund* (DGB), so that the interests of different industries tend to cancel out. The attitude of the individual unions is shown by their reaction, in the mid-1970s, to ideas of 'structural policy', advocated by a section of the Social Democratic Party. Some trade union economists, speaking for industries with serious problems, supported ideas of structural policy, but this was not an agreed view of the DGB as a whole. Although the unions were not hostile to proposals to establish industrial councils, they gave priority to their efforts to seek greater influence via union representation on the boards of individual enterprises.[17]

For many years, the unions were brought together with representatives of management and government in the tripartite framework of 'Concerted Action'. This was largely a forum for consideration of general economic conditions as a framework for wage bargaining. The unions pulled out of 'Concerted Action' in 1977. The proximate cause was the action by the employers in referring the codetermination law to the Federal Constitutional Court, though the unions were also dissatisfied at the narrow scope of the tripartite discussions.

POLITICAL PRESSURES ON POLICY-MAKERS

The German government is of course subjected, like others, to sectional pressures. When in 1976 a mission from the Japanese Keidanren (the representative organ for big business) visited Western Europe, they received a lecture from an official in Bonn about Japanese exports, 'as if we had returned to Britain'. They were told that Japanese exports of ships, steel and bearings had become a political issue, orderly marketing arrangements being ineffective. 'Every day', requests were coming in from German industries for protection against imports from Japan.[18] In March 1980, the German electronics firms called for restraints on Japanese exports for two to three years.[19]

Such pressures from industry are to be expected. Where Germany differs from other Community countries, such as France, Italy and the United Kingdom (particularly under Labour governments), is in the strength of the central orthodoxy that protection and subsidies are deviations from sound rules of policy. It is sometimes suggested that the Germans enjoy a public posture of ideological purity while privately welcoming protection forced upon them by their Community partners. No doubt individual German industries welcome such protection; but it is hardly to be thought that Count Lambsdorff was hypocritical when, for example, he vigorously opposed the tightening up of protection of Community producers of textiles and clothing under the Multifibre Arrangement in 1977 and again in 1981. Indeed, there are indications that Germany did not insist on rigorous observance of the textile quotas negotiated in 1977 as did other Community countries.[20] In 1982–3, Count Lambsdorff resisted the negotiation by Commissioner Davignon of export restraint agreements for Japanese video cassette recorders and other items. On the other hand, it was reported that in 1980 he had given the Japanese 'friendly advice' to exercise restraint, especially for cars.[21] Certainly, despite the force of the liberal orthodoxy, some industries have benefited from close links with particular ministers or ministries. Indeed, some observers maintain that industrial interests have more influence with the CDU/CSU coalition than with the previous government when the SPD was the major partner.

INTER-MINISTERIAL COORDINATION

While Germany, often with support from the Netherlands and Denmark, has tended to take a free-market attitude in matters of Community trade and industrial policy, it has not been notably successful in influencing the outcome. This lack of success is sometimes attributed to difficulty, within the German government machine, of reaching an agreed, unified view which can then be forcefully presented. It is observed that Germany tends to send large delegations to international meetings as each ministry with an interest in the proceedings wishes to send its own representative. The autonomy given to the various ministers by the constitution appears to make for certain problems of coordination. On the other hand, the wide span of responsibility of the Economics Ministry enables many issues in trade and industrial policy to be settled within one ministry. At the same time, the Foreign Ministry takes an active role in matters of cooperation within the Community and this has been bolstered since 1972, by the coordinating role, for Community questions, of a Minister of State in the Foreign Ministry. While subordinate to the Foreign Minister, this Minister of State is a member of the Cabinet, so that he can present the details of policy decisions which require approval at the highest level.[22] Various sections of the Foreign Ministry follow questions of international economic relations arising both in the Community and elsewhere.

There are four standing inter-ministerial committees dealing with Community matters. Everyday matters are dealt with by the Committee for the Preparation of the German Permanent Representation at the EEC, commonly known as the Tuesday Committee. This is a working-level group, chaired by an official from the Economics Ministry. Still at the specialist level, and also chaired by an official from the Economics Ministry, is the Group of European Specialists. This deals mainly with longer-term issues. The Committee for European Affairs of State Secretaries (official heads of the relevant ministries) meets monthly. Its main task is to prepare for meetings of the Community Council of Foreign Ministers, though it also meets *ad hoc* on occasions. It is chaired by the Minister of State at the Foreign Ministry with responsibility for coordination of community affairs and attended by a senior official from the Chancellor's office; other State Secretaries attend according to the subject matter. Finally, a European Committee of the Federal Cabinet was instituted in March 1985. It is chaired by the Chancellor or acting Chancellor (or, in their absence, by the Foreign Minister). The other permanent members are the Ministers of Economics, Finance, and Food, Agriculture and Forests.

The role of the Chancellor's Office in Community questions varies according to the current interest of the Chancellor himself. Its main task is to prepare working papers to keep the Chancellor and his close advisers informed of developments in the Community. It has no policy-making functions in its own right.[23]

There appears to be no lack of coordinating machinery within the Federal government machine. If in the past Germany failed to 'punch its weight' in the Community, this would appear to be for some other reason. Until the early 1980s, German representatives tended to back down in the event of conflicts in the Community, particularly in conflicts with France (a tendency which French negotiators are said to have exploited). Germany backed away from a strongly argued position in the run up to the extension of the Multifibre Arrangement in

1977. It gave way again over the institution of steel quotas in the Community in 1980; and again during the carbon steel negotiation with the United States in 1982, even though German steel producers would have been better off without an agreement and had a very strong case. An element in this case, however, may have been fear of increased competition in the domestic market from subsidised producers elsewhere in the Community. On the other hand, in the discussion of the Community's New Commercial Policy Instrument in 1984, Germany together with the United Kingdom defeated France by insisting that decisions to use this instrument should be taken by qualified majority vote of the Council. The German government, though, would have preferred not to establish the New Commercial Policy Instrument at all, but lacked the requisite support for this position.

German officials maintained that the national position was based essentially on a calculation of voting strength in the Community. As has been seen in Chapter 3, if in the Community of ten countries, the German position was supported only by the Netherlands and Denmark, these three countries were not sufficient to block a qualified majority in the Council. Nevertheless, it might appear that Germany's interest in the question of steel quotas and in the negotiations with the United States over carbon steel would have been enough to justify a veto under the Luxembourg Compromise on grounds of a very important national interest.

In addition to their tendency, at any rate until recently, to compromise national positions, German representatives in Community bodies are commonly said to have lacked skill and pertinacity as negotiators. It is said that, after making strong opening statements in favour of liberal policy, they tended not to follow through.

In more recent years, however, the German government has been increasingly willing to stand up for its own position in the Community, even if it has found itself in a minority of one or two. One example was the German linkage in 1984, in the face of French opposition, of an increase in the Community's budgetary 'own resources' on the one hand and the accession of Spain and Portugal on the other. In 1985, the German government pursued, in isolation, a line on standards for vehicle emissions which made them very unpopular with their larger Community partners. It is also interesting to note that after German representatives had persistently asserted their dislike of the right of veto under the Luxembourg Compromise, in 1985 the German Minister of Agriculture invoked the Luxembourg

Compromise to block the Commission's proposals on cereal prices and exchange rates for agricultural goods. Since reunification in 1990, observers have detected an increased assertiveness by German spokesmen, conscious that they represent by far the largest country of the Community in terms of population.

SUMMARY

It has been seen that, in Germany, a conscious decision after the war to follow free-market economic policies has been bolstered – at any rate as concerns manufacturing industry – by two mass parties competing for the political middle ground and by various institutional arrangements. These include the powers of the Economics Ministry, corporatist relations with summit organisations representing economic interests, a technocratic approach to issues of economic policy in parliamentary committees and the role of the banks in assisting industrial restructuring. (There are, nevertheless, various exceptions to the free-market approach, even in manufacturing, and very much more in agriculture and services). In the Community, German representatives have tended to oppose protectionist measures for manufactured goods. Their opposition has often been unsuccessful, however, not only because they were in a minority in the Community, but also because of their reluctance to push differences of opinion – particularly with the French authorities – beyond a certain point. Another possible reason for their lack of success in thwarting protectionist measures is the problem of coordination resulting from the provision in the constitution for the 'autonomy' of the various ministers.

   In the next chapter, it will be seen that in France both the climate of ideas and the effects of the institutional arrangements are very different.

7 Making Trade Policy in France

In matters of Community trade policy, France has commonly been at the opposite pole from Germany, calling for protection where Germany (often with the support of the Netherlands and Denmark) has opposed it. In the words of an experienced British trade negotiator: 'When we or the Germans protect, we feel guilty about it. The French do not'.

A *DIRIGISTE* APPROACH

The conventional picture of French economic policy is of a strong *dirigiste* tradition, carried out by the dominant executive branch of the government, supported by an able technocratic civil service and buttressed by an informal network of ministers, officials, industrialists and bankers, many of them the products of the same élite technical universities (*grandes écoles*).

This picture is nearer the truth than many such stereotypes. It is still necessary, however, to ask to what extent French trade policy and other policies related to trade are shaped by a body of ideas and the institutional heritage and to what extent by particular political pressure. Moreover, account must be taken of the movement towards more market-oriented policies which occurred in 1983 and was reinforced by the electoral swing from a socialist to a conservative majority in 1986.

This chapter considers in turn:

(a) certain manifestations of French trade policy in recent years;
(b) ideas which have influenced policy, and the features of the French situation which have made for a *dirigiste* approach;
(c) the evolution of French trade and industrial policies over the years since World War II;
(d) institutional arrangements affecting policy;
(e) political pressures on policy makers;
(f) arrangements for coordination of policy on Community matters.

SOME FACETS OF FRENCH TRADE POLICY

Successive French governments have been at the protectionist end of opinion in the Community, advocating protectionist policies by the Community as a whole and being prepared on occasions to take unilateral action, in defiance at least of the spirit of Community law. A few examples will illustrate this.

First, in 1977 the French authorities were in the forefront of those pressing for tighter restrictions on imports of textiles and clothing under the Multifibre Arrangement. In June 1977, the French government notified the Commission of its intention to take unilateral action to impose quantitative restrictions on imports of various textiles and clothing items from low-income countries. This step, immediately challenged on grounds of Community law by the Commission, was no doubt intended in large part to force the Commission's hand in negotiating provisions which would allow the tightening up of restrictive agreements with supplying countries. In the following month, the French Foreign Minister protested to Commissioner Haferkamp, the Commissioner responsible for DG I (International Relations), that in the negotiation for the extension of the MFA the Commission was accepting forms of words which were not in accord with the directive laid down by the Council.

Also in 1977, the French authorities took steps to limit imports of cars from Japan to 3 per cent of the French market. This arrangement is more restrictive than the United Kingdom's inter-industry agreement, though less restrictive than the long-standing quantitative restrictions which exist in Italy.[1]

Third, in 1982 the French Minister of the Budget sought to limit imports of video cassette recorders from all sources by decreeing that they should be channelled through the small customs post of Poitiers. When the Commission declared this arrangement to be impermissible under Community law, the French authorities adopted monitoring arrangements allowing the foreign trade minister to prevent 'excessive' imports.

The protectionist nature of French trade policy can also be discerned from the fact that in the early 1980s the French authorities pressed for the adoption of the Community's New Commercial Policy Instrument, designed to facilitate action against illicit commercial practices by countries outside the Community. Similarly, in 1985, President Mitterrand blocked Community agreement to a date for the start of a new GATT negotiating round, on the grounds that the preparations which had been made at that time did not adequately protect certain Community (and French) interests.

The French position on Community trade policy in the early 1980s was shown by the French Government's memorandum, *A New Step for Europe: A Common Industrial and Research Area*, sent to the Council of the European Communities in September 1983. While this is largely about industrial policy, it also contains statements on trade. For example:

> The common market is a very open commercial area, with nearly 50% of the EEC's imports being made free of duty. . . . As a general rule, this opening up of the EEC is especially beneficial since it ferments competition. It is essential to maintain it.

The document continues:

> This does not mean, however, that the European industrial area should merge entirely and without any limitation into the world industrial area, nor are the trade practices of our major competitors conducive to this. Commercial policy must, as far as necessary and while complying with the Community's international commitments, contribute to the Community's new industrial strategy. Such has been the case for certain sectors in difficulty. The same should certainly apply to certain sectors of the future if the birth and early development of industries with a bright future are to be made easier. A significant, if temporary, increase in customs duties must be possible where it can effectively encourage the emergence of a European industry, as has been already requested by one Member State in the case of launching of a European 'compact disc' manufacturing programme . . .

The memorandum proposes that preference in public procurement should be given to 'Community producers'. Moreover, it also states that:

> In order to eliminate the abuse of the free movement of products said to be of Community origin but which in reality are only an assembly of imported products, the current definition of "Community product" should be clarified. Loopholes in the common external tariff are unacceptable.

While many of the ideas in the memorandum as a whole were widely acceptable, the proposals on trade policy were rejected not only by the German authorities but also by those of the United Kingdom.

IDEAS AND ATTITUDES INFLUENCING TRADE POLICY

Two questions are considered in this section: (i) to what extent French trade policy has been based on a coherent framework of ideas; and (ii) why it is these ideas that have been influential in France and not, for example, the decidedly different ideas that have influenced policy in Germany.

Ideas on Policy

Foreign trade is hardly recognised in France as a subject for systematic thought and analysis. It appears that the theory of comparative cost and other staple concepts of trade theory are not taught in French universities.

Responses to a questionnaire, sent to economists in France, Belgium, Switzerland, Germany and the United States, showed significant differences in economic thinking between economists educated in the French tradition and those educated in the United States and Germany. The economists were asked whether they 'generally agree', 'agree with provisions' or 'generally disagree' with various macro- and micro-economic propositions. Only 27 per cent of French respondents and 32 per cent of the Belgians 'generally agreed' with the proposition that tariffs and import quotas reduce general economic welfare, against 49 per cent of the Swiss, 70 per cent of the Germans, and 81 per cent of the Americans. Only 12 per cent of the French and 17 per cent of the Belgians thought that flexible exchange rates offer an effective international monetary arrangement, against 53 per cent of the Swiss, 64 per cent of the Germans and 61 per cent of the Americans.[2]

Despite the comparative neglect of foreign trade as a subject of study in France, at least three major books wholly or largely concerned with trade policy have been published in France in recent years.

(a) *Pour un Nouveau Protectionnisme*, written by Jean-Marcel Jean-neney, who was the Minister for Industry under President de

Gaulle from 1959 to 1962, Minister for Social Affairs from 1966 to 1968 and Minister of State from 1968 to 1969;[3] the book was published in 1978.

(b) *La Grande Menace industrielle*, also published in 1978, by Christian Stoffaës, subsequently an official in the Ministry of Industry.[4]

(c) *Le Commerce international à la dérive*, by François David, subsequently a senior official in the Department of External Economic Relations;[5] this book was published in 1982.

There are differences of opinion as to the influence of Jeanneney's book. One senior official in early 1986 dismissed Jeanneney as 'a nostalgic Gaullist'. Nevertheless, the central proposition in the book appears to have been important in French thinking: that a country, or the Community, should choose its own economic structure. 'One would not be able to accept free trade without asking whether there is a risk that it will prevent the realisation of the desired structure.'[6] Jeanneney concludes that the protectionist policies, which he advocates, should be operated at the level of the Community as a whole. This should involve strengthening the Community's decision-making power.

Among the arguments advanced by Jeanneney in favour of his 'new protectionism' are the following:

(a) A wide variety of types of production makes the fullest use of an area's human and natural potential.[7]

(b) It allows useful linkages of supply and demand and provides a variety of examples on which managements can draw.[8]

(c) There is no guarantee that new activities will spring up to provide employment suited to the skills of workers displaced by increased imports.[9]

(d) A wide variety of types of production avoids excessive unevenness in the geographical distribution of activity (certainly a significant strand in French thinking in the past).[10]

(e) Variety also reduces cyclical fluctuations, because of the different timing of variations in demand for different products. Specialisation in production of capital goods leads to particular problems of fluctuation of demand.[11]

(f) It is important to protect oneself against foreign attempts at dominance or blackmail (another significant strand in French thinking).[12]

Stoffaës in his book also saw dangers in unregulated international economic interdependence. Most specifically, he feared that, without active industrial and trade policies, France would fall progressively further behind the advanced industrial countries while being hotly pursued by the newly-industrialising countries of Southern Europe, Latin America and South-East Asia.[13]

More generally, he saw a threat to the country's preferred way of life:

> when an economy works as to 25 per cent or more for the outside world, as is the case for a growing number of Western countries, it is not only the economic cycle or the rate of interest which can no longer be fixed to reflect domestic needs. The organisation of society, the way of life, cultural values, also have to be aligned on the external model. Economic interdependence brings with it a type of organisation which, for thirty years, has been largely derived from the United States model. Is it necessary now, in order to win the competitive battle with the Japanese, to adopt their way of life and methods of organisation and to set out to resemble them? . . . [Moreover] ways of life are transmitted by liberal trade since the exporting countries impose on their customers products originally conceived for themselves.[14]

Stoffaës, like Jeanneney, was concerned at problems in particular parts of the country. He pointed out that the North and Lorraine were experiencing a continuing adjustment crisis in textiles, mining and steel-making. The areas which would benefit from the growth of markets in developing countries were almost the inverse of those which would suffer from increased international competition. 'Except for the Paris region and the Rhône-Alps area, where structural change is easy, the least sectoral difficulty endangers local employment and sets off political and trade union pressures in favour of defensive choices.'[15]

As to the international trading system in general, he further argues that liberal trade theory is falsified by the intervention of governments for a variety of economic, political and social reasons. This could lead to a situation which is unfavourable to all, so that 'global planning, agreement among nations, are better able than simple competition to bring improvements for all partners at once'.[16]

François David in his book was concerned to show that 60 per cent of international trade is subject to regulation in one form or another.

Writing under time-pressure, he specifically denied the intention 'to propose solutions to the crisis in international commercial relations'. He suggested, however, that the widespread regulation of trade 'is an element which governments and economic agents should integrate into their strategies.'[17]

In parallel with concern for the economic well-being of the different parts of the country, a strand in French policy-making has been concern for the 'small man'. As part of their quest for political legitimacy and support, political parties from the extreme left to the extreme right have consistently declared their desire to protect the 'small saver', the 'small shopkeeper', the 'small businessman', the 'small farmer'.[18] This concern, in uneasy double-harness with the desire to modernise the economy, has led to dualism in economic policy and this mirrors the continuing dualism in the economic structure of the country.

Internationally, French policy has shown an anxious concern for national independence, accompanied by a continuing streak of anti-Americanism. These attitudes appear to have been reinforced by certain traumatic experiences – for example, the refusal by President Johnson in 1966 to allow exports of electronic equipment needed for French rockets. This led directly to the '*Plan Calcul*' to build up the French computer industry.[19]

There would appear to have been rather little attention given in France to the arguments against protection and subsidisation, that they impose costs on the remainder of the economy and that they may well discourage necessary adjustment and restructuring. A senior official dealing with trade policy in France said that no studies had been made there of the costs of protection and that there was no demand for such studies.

APPEAL OF INTERVENTIONIST POLICIES

Arguments supporting interventionist policies readily appeal to the élite group of politicians, officials, industrial managers and bankers in France trained in a certain tradition of public service in the *grandes écoles*.[20]

One of the first acts of President de Gaulle after World War II was to set up the École Nationale d'Administration (ENA) to train the high officials of the future. It has been observed that present-day technocrats who have been trained in the *grandes écoles* acknowledge the rules of an administrative law the principles of which were determined centuries ago. The basic tenet is that there is a 'general interest' which is above particular interests. Only the state can determine what the general interest is and the state alone must defend it.[21]

The dominant role of the *grandes écoles* in educating the senior officials of the future has produced an élite which spreads through the French system. The members of this élite share a common indoctrination even though they differ in their political views. There is a less distinct boundary in the French system than in the British between Ministers and many of the senior officials. President Giscard d'Estaing, and many Prime Ministers and other Ministers, have themselves been products of the ENA.

Giscard d'Estaing and other prominent political figures served as officials earlier in their careers. Also, many senior officials move across into high management positions in industry and finance (a practice so general as to be known in common parlance as *pantouflage*, 'putting on slippers'). The paternalistic approach to government is deeply entrenched. Thus Simon Nora, the head of ENA, has been quoted as saying that his students 'now believe that it is the state's job to teach the country to be more liberal.'[22]

Many commentators see *dirigiste* economic policies in France as a natural offshoot of a concern for the strength of the state and of the central government. Through the series of revolutions from 1789 onwards, and other political vicissitudes such as the need for a fresh start after World War II:

> successive French regimes have regarded the legitimacy of their authority as questionable, the monolithic character of the political and administrative state apparatus being necessary to coerce into a semblance of consensus and order the disparate and divided fragments of the national mosaic.[23]

· The institutional framework, and its effects on the making of trade policy, will be considered in more detail after the following survey of the evolution of trade and industrial policies over the post-war years.

DEVELOPMENTS IN TRADE AND INDUSTRIAL POLICY

French actions in the field of international trade, to the extent that they do not simply spring from particular political pressures, have been offshoots of industrial policy (which has itself passed through several phases since World War II). Indeed, to some considerable extent French trade policy has been not merely an adjunct to industrial policy but also a response to its failures.

The circumstances of France immediately after World War II favoured the emergence of a system of government economic planning. Business leaders had been discredited by collaboration with the Vichy regime, while labour interests drew strength from identification with the Resistance.

> The Plan . . . was initiated with support from labor, survived despite the resistance of business, and then evolved into a mechanism for collaboration between business and the state.[24]

The first post-war phase involved the building up of the instruments of government intervention and the channelling of funds to sectors considered essential to post-war reconstruction. At the same time, in order to retain adequate political support, the governments of the time had to perform a careful balancing act between the modern and traditional sectors. While one set of policies aimed to promote and organise the forces of change in the economy, another set was designed to reduce opposition from those threatened in the process.[25]

A second phase of industrial policy can be said to have begun in 1959, with the second accession to the Presidency of General de Gaulle and the coming into operation of the European Community. The emphasis was on prestige projects such as the Concorde airliner and the establishment of a colour television system, on mergers, and on the establishment of large 'national champion' firms. In sectors such as electronics and steel, state intervention kept alive firms which would otherwise have perished before they could adjust to the new competitive environment. Interventionist policies were bolstered, then and later, by the importance of governmental financial institutions.[26]

After a few years it became apparent that technocratic errors had led to much costly misdirection of resources, producing new problems without resolving the old ones. The technocrats came to have less confidence in their prescience; and at this point there came the first oil price shock of 1973–4.

The third phase of industrial policy began with the election to the Presidency of Valéry Giscard d'Estaing in 1974. The rhetoric of this period was liberal, though there are differences of opinion on the actual balance between liberalism and *dirigisme*.[27] Price controls were removed, and there was an increased emphasis on the need for internationally competitive firms. Even during the premiership of Raymond Barre (1976–81), an avowed economic liberal, the government continued to use subsidies, cheap loans, favourable depreciation allowances, research grants, development contracts and public procurement to promote such activities as robotics, biotechnology, information technology and energy-saving. Mergers were promoted in steel, heavy chemicals, shipbuilding, the car industry, textiles and telecommunication equipment.

The successive phases of industrial policy did not succeed in making the major French industries internationally competitive. As already noted, in 1977 the French government took steps to limit imports of Japanese cars and to protect the textile and clothing industries, first through unilateral measures and subsequently through the tightening up of restraints under the Multifibre Arrangement.

In 1981, the socialist President Mitterrand came to power, pledged on the one hand to extend the nationalised sector of the French economy and, on the other hand, to decentralise political decision-making.

In the preceding years, industrial policy had become the subject of a major political debate, a relatively new phenomenon in French politics.

> In opposition, the left had reproached the Government for leading France into de-industrialization and under-employment, far too easily accepting 'market forces' and the international division of labour – in short, for a policy of 'abandon'.[28]

The new Socialist government started off as interventionist and expansionist. Newly nationalised banks were to provide the finance for expansion of the industrial sector. Jean-Pierre Chevènement (Minister of Industry, 1982–3) confirmed a policy of *filières*, the building up of vertically integrated chains of production, as against the alternative policy of *créneaux*, the search for niches in the international market in which France could enjoy actual or potential comparative advantage. The slogan was introduced of 'reconquest of the domestic market'.

The policies of the new government rapidly ran into acute problems – loss of foreign confidence in the franc and accelerating inflation at home. One faction – nicknamed 'the Albanians' – pressed for a policy of increased autarky, including a break with the European

Monetary System (EMS). President Mitterrand, however, opted for solutions within the framework of the Community, including continued membership of the EMS. This had far-reaching consequences for economic policy. Domestic expansion gave rise to policies of 'rigour' in March 1982 and 'increased rigour' in March 1983 as noted in Chapter 4. Within the framework of Community membership, greatly increased protection as advocated by 'the Albanians' was not feasible. The change of policy was accompanied by major changes in the composition of the government.

The need for a major change of course in macro-economic policy went hand-in-hand with new attitudes to micro-economic policy. The policy of *filières* had proved impossible to implement in practice. It was recognised that many of the best prospects for the future lay with small and medium-sized firms, and hence with decentralised decision-making. Laurent Fabius, who became Prime Minister in the summer of 1984, declared: 'The state has come up against its limits: it should not go beyond them'.[29] There was increased recognition of the importance of exports to the French economy, and a wide range of firms, small as well as large, were interested in selling in world markets. Increased weight was given to the risk that protection – even in the framework of the Multifibre Arrangement – might lead to retaliation, limiting export possibilities.

The Gaullist constitution of the Fifth Republic envisaged a Prime Minister acting in close cooperation with an active, policy-making President. This arrangement was called into question with the election, in March 1986, of a rightist majority in the Chamber of Deputies, while the Socialist François Mitterrand remained President. The ideology of the new majority together with divided counsels at the centre, reinforced the trend toward less interventionist economic policies. Nevertheless, several commentators noted that the élite network of the products of the *grandes écoles* does not easily abandon its *dirigiste* habits of thought; and close observers state that there was no apparent change in French official attitudes to matters of Community trade policy – although the French see potential advantages in liberalisation of trade in some services. From 1988, there was once again a Socialist Prime Minister under a Socialist President.

INSTITUTIONAL ARRANGEMENTS

Institutional features affecting the making of trade policy are:

(a) the great strength of the executive under the constitution;
(b) the comparative weakness of parliament in influencing policy;
(c) close institutional and personal links whereby local pressures are
     brought to bear on the central government.

Strength of the Executive

The challenge to the unity of the republic arising in 1958 over the war
in Algeria provided a welcome opportunity to 'restore the state' by
reverting to the Napoleonic concentration of power in the hands of
the President and reduction of the power of parliament.[30] Under the
constitution of the Fifth Republic, drawn up by General de Gaulle,
the President has power to appoint the Prime Minister and to dissolve
the legislature. The *Chambre des Députés* (the lower house of parliament) can force the Prime Minister to resign following a vote of
censure, but the President could then dissolve the Chamber and force
a general election, should he so choose.

Clearly, the concentration of power vested in the President and a
Prime Minister appointed by him is less strong when, as was the case
between 1986 and 1988, the President and Prime Minister are of
different political persuasions. This situation might appear to increase
the influence of parliament through its power to force the Prime
Minister's resignation. In the early days of his premiership, however,
Jacques Chirac (Prime Minister 1986–88) was able to sidestep problems with his coalition partners by using the emergency powers in the
constitution to issue decrees.[31]

Ministers enjoy strongly politicised support in the exercise of their
functions. First, each has his own personal staff (*cabinet*) made up, at
the minister's discretion, of both political appointees and officials,
typically chosen to put a wide range of experience and contacts at the
Ministers' disposal. Second, political appointments are usual, not
only in the Ministers' *cabinets*, but even down to middling levels in
the civil service (though many of these appointments are of already
established civil servants). Moreover, there has been an increasing
tendency for even career civil servants to be identified with one or
other political group or figure.

Since 1974, there has been a post of Minister of External Trade.
The hierarchical position of the French trade minister has gone
through various changes – an illustration perhaps of the uncertain
status of trade policy in French thinking.

When Michel Jobert was Minister of Trade, from 1981 to 1983, he held senior cabinet rank on a personal basis, but had to rely for official advice on departments which were not under his direct command. It appears that the decision in 1982 that imported video cassette recorders must be cleared through the small customs post in Poitiers was taken by Laurent Fabius, Minister of the Budget, without consulting other ministers; M. Jobert first heard of the decision over the radio. He resigned in 1983, complaining that the administrative arrangements did not allow him to carry out a 'coherent and effective policy'.[32]

Under the various hierarchical arrangements, successive trade ministers have been able to look for support from the Department of External Economic Relations (DREE), a department of the Ministry of the Economy, Finance and the Budget. Up to 1983 the DREE was largely concerned with export credit policy, but in response to the balance of payments crisis it was then given responsibility for import policy; it has also provided the French representatives to the Article 113 Committee.

Edith Cresson became trade minister in 1983 on a similar basis to her precursor; but in 1984 she was appointed Minister for Industrial Redeployment and External Trade, thus bringing together responsibilities for trade and industry. In the Chirac government (1986–8), the Trade Minister was subordinate to the Finance Minister. In the Rocard administration which came to power in mid-1988, the Trade Minister once again reported directly to the Prime Minister and had no body of officials directly under his control, though he was advised by DREE and other departments.

The officials concerned with trade policy feel themselves to be in a strong position, *vis-à-vis* their minister, by reason of the technical and detailed nature of the subject matter. Of recent Trade Ministers, only Jean-François Deniau (who held the post from 1978 to 1980) had any considerable relevant background, although others – notably Michel Jobert – took strong positions on matters of policy from time to time.

Limited Influence of Parliament

The French parliament has intervened rather little in matters of trade policy. For example, years can pass without a debate on trade policy as such. By the constitution, ministers may not be members of parliament though they are responsible to it. They seldom attend parliamentary debates except to preserve their Bills and their shares of the budget. The constitution limits parliamentary sessions to less than six months of the year. The government is firmly in charge of parliamentary business: there are no occasions for opposition parties to raise questions for debate, except by putting down a full-blown censure motion. Nevertheless, the annual discussion of a minister's budget gives deputies the opportunity to make points or raise issues.[33] Parliamentary questions on trade matters have been few and far between.

Although every government bill must be sent to a parliamentary committee, the committee is not allowed to make counter-proposals which depart from the government's intent. The committee must report to the Chamber within three months or even sooner if the government has labelled the bill as urgent (and on occasion bills have come up for debate before the committee had had time to prepare its report or even, in extreme cases, to discuss them at all). *Ad hoc* parliamentary committees of inquiry into government operations are limited by set time-periods and narrow terms of reference. Their membership is selected by vote of the majority, which may exclude Deputies likely to be interested in embarrassing the government.[34]

Despite the comparative weakness of parliament under the French constitution. there is word of mouth testimony that producer groups devote a fair amount of effort to lobbying Deputies, and this suggests that the Deputies are by no means without influence in matters of trade and industrial policy (including influence exercised through informal contacts).[35]

POLITICAL PRESSURES ON POLICY-MAKERS

It has been seen that the constitution of the Fifth Republic drastically reduces the power of the parliament as against that of the executive. In general, French governments are more concerned about votes in the next general election than with parliamentary pressures.[36]

· A study of the influence ot pressure groups under the Fifth Republic concluded that France is closer to the pluralist than to the corporatist model.[37] The Economic and Social Council, made up of representatives of government and of economic peak organisations, is generally considered to have been relatively ineffective. The *Conseil National du Patronat Français* (the '*Patronat*'), however, is by no means without influence. Although membership is far from homogeneous, it includes the directors of nationalised industries and of other firms highly dependent on government as well as directors of companies with a more independent approach. A rival body is the *Confédération Général des Petites et Moyennes Entreprises*. Nationalised and other large firms have a considerable influence behind the scenes, aided by the migration of ex-officials into industry and finance as well as into politics.

The trade unions also exert influence, though they are less strong than those in the United Kingdom. In the first place, the level of unionisation in France has been among the lowest in Europe. One estimate put actual membership at about 20 per cent of potential membership, after allowing for the inflation of membership claims with a declining trend.[38] Moreover, the unions are weakened by fragmentation and intense rivalry between different groups: there are five major national confederations, plus dozens of smaller, autonomous unions based on a single region, industry or firm. Demonstrations by workers are so frequent that they are pretty much taken for granted. Some commentators see them as the protests of the powerless. Moreover, such direct action is difficult to organise from the top and it usually emerges from the rank and file. 'The inability of the trade union leadership to control the use or avoidance of such activity reduces the political impact that these protests might have on policy.'[39]

Some authors see a tendency for the French authorities to try to insulate themselves from interest groups. For example, Professor Hayward of Hull University considers that:

By multiplying consultative committees whose powerlessness means that they are unlikely to resolve conflicts, the government encourages each sectional interest to respond to its unilateral decisions by uncompromising obstruction, which only confirms the government in its belief that change has to be imposed.[40]

Another view that has been expressed puts forward the thesis that:

French bureaucrats, with their highly developed sense that they alone represent the public interest, view excessive involvement of interest groups in the decision-making process as endangering both democracy and the 'objective' resolution of a problem. As the civil servants' principle aim is to obtain information, and not necessarily to listen to advice, they tend to make a distinction between pressure groups, which they view as harmful, and professional associations, which have expertise and are equipped to interpret the bureaucracy's activities to the outside.[41]

The same author goes on to assert that:

an interest group today has greater legitimation and more secure access to the public authorities if its basic aims are roughly in accordance with, or encapsulated in, the policy orientations of the executive.[42]

Nevertheless, concern with the industrial future of the country leads to fairly close contact between officials and certain producer interests – facilitated, in some cases, by the 'old-boy network' of graduates from the *grandes écoles*. In some cases, indeed, the authorities have been disappointed by the inability of industry groups to state clear preferences on policy alternatives.[43] By comparison, there has been little or no receptivity to importer and consumer interests.

Two features of the French system enable pressures from the various regions and localities of the country to be brought to bear on central government. In the first place, the same individual may occupy key offices at the communal level (as mayor), the department level (as councillor or president of the departmental council) and the national level (as deputy, senator or minister). This arrangement is facilitated by the restricted length of parliamentary sessions. A more recent law limits the number of public posts which may be held by a single person; but it is still common, for example, for a minister or a member of the Chamber of Deputies also to be mayor of a commune somewhere in France.

Secondly, the prefects, while first and foremost the agents of the central government in the provinces (*départements*), became the advocates of local interests: to operate effectively they needed the support of such people as the local mayors and departmental councillors and to win this support they had to act as advocates of local interests with the central government.

In recent years, nevertheless, with macro-economic problems and changes in the pattern of economic activity resulting from technological changes as well as from international competition, it has no longer been possible to bolster up economic activity in some of the worst-affected areas. Moreover, the measures of decentralisation make the regions more obviously responsible for their own destinies.

Nevertheless, the political pressures for central government actions to safeguard the interests of the various regions of the country remain strong.

COORDINATION

A number of ministries have interests in matters of trade policy – notably the Ministries of Industry, Agriculture, the Economy and Finance, and Foreign Affairs. The central responsibility for coordination in all policy matters lies with the government's general secretariat in the Prime Minister's office. Under this, the Interministerial Committee for Questions of European Economic Cooperation has coordinating responsibility for all Community matters. Any statement of French government policy (such as the 1983 Memorandum, *A New Step for Europe: a Common Industrial and Research Area*) has to be cleared through this machinery.

Some observers stress that the French administration is made up of a number of warring fiefdoms (even divisions within ministries), and that overall coordination is erratic.[44] The Poitiers affair supports this view. It appears that the international implications were considered only after the order had been given.

A considerable responsibility rests with the general secretariat to try to detect matters on which there should be inter-ministerial coordination and to organise this coordination. At the same time, if a minister feels that he is being left out of the discussion of a matter in which he has a legitimate interest, he may make representations to the Prime Minister's office that he should be consulted.

It appears that trade matters would not normally be discussed by a committee of ministers. Inter-ministerial discussions may take place at various levels of seniority, or between members of the ministers' *cabinets*. Much coordination is carried out in informal *ad hoc* ways. The *cabinets* play an important part in the working of the machinery of government, together with the (overlapping) informal network of the ex-students of the *grandes écoles*.[45]

Such failures of coordination as there may be do not prevent French representatives from expressing strong views on matters of Community trade policy; but they may call into question the extent to which these views represent agreement between all the parts of the central government with a legitimate interest.

SUMMARY

In France, the government insecurity engendered by successive revolutions in the past has contributed to the building up of a strong
executive; this is particularly so in the constitution of the Fifth Republic. Moreover, the upper levels of politics, the administration and
business are permeated by graduates of the *École Nationale d'Administration* and other élite training institutions (*hautes écoles*), indoctrinated with paternalist and *dirigiste* ideas.

There has been little emphasis in economic education in France on
the theory of the potential gains from international trade. This,
together with continuing preoccupation with national independence,
has led to an emphasis on the idea that a country (or the Community
as a whole) should determine its own preferred economic structure
and not allow the pattern of activity to be shaped by the forces of
international competition.

Political circumstances at the end of World War II favoured the
adoption of national economic planning. The duality of the French
economy, in which modern and traditional activities have conspicuously existed side by side, has led to a corresponding duality in government economic policies. Concern to maintain the economic bases of
the different parts of the country has been reinforced by the nature of
the institutional links between local areas and the centre.

To some extent, French governments have resorted to, or pressed
for, protection in response to failures of past interventionist policies.
From 1983, the lessons of experience led to a more market-oriented
approach to internal economic policy, but this made little perceptible
difference to French attitudes to trade policy.

8 Making Trade Policy in the United Kingdom

Until the early 1980s, the policies of successive governments in the United Kingdom on imports of manufactures tended to be nearer to the French than to the German position. Apart from the issue of nationalisation and denationalisation, the industrial and trade policies followed by successive Conservative and Labour governments were more similar than might be expected given the differences in their stated principles and their electoral support. Trade policies could be described as pragmatic, with considerable emphasis on consideration of the votes to be won or lost.

The election in 1979 of a Conservative government under the premiership of Mrs Margaret Thatcher did not, for several years, make any very noticeable difference to trade policy in spite of the avowedly free-market principles of the government. In the second half of the 1980s and early 1990s, however, there were increasing signs of resistance to the more protectionist forces in the Community.

The position of the United Kingdom could be said to lie midway between the protectionist and liberal wings of the Community countries. Various protectionist actions by the United Kingdom have been noted in Chapter 2; but, across the board, the United Kingdom has been less protectionist than France. In 1985 it supported the opening of a new round of multilateral trade negotiations in the GATT, against resistance from the French government; and in the early 1990s the British authorities have favoured a generally liberal outcome to the Uruguay Round.

In this chapter, the following aspects of trade policy in the United Kingdom will be examined:

(a) the major influences on policy;
(b) the development of trade and industrial policies over the post-war years;
(c) the institutional framework and its effects on policy making;
(d) the political pressures on policy makers;
(e) the arrangements which exist in the UK system for coordination of policy on questions arising in the Community.

MAJOR INFLUENCES ON TRADE POLICY

The prevailing orthodoxy in the United Kingdom, as taught in universities, stresses the potential gains from unrestricted international trade. Even the 'New Cambridge' group of economists, although they advocated restriction of the total value of imports in order to allow expansion of the domestic economy while escaping from the balance-of-payments constraint, emphasised that this control should be administered on a non-discriminatory basis in order to avoid economic distortions.

In the early post-war years, officials dealing with trade policy followed a generally liberal approach; they felt themselves to be identified with the founding of the GATT. In the 1970s, there was a shift among officials to a more pragmatic approach, in parallel with the rise of protectionist pressures at political level. Two senior officials working in the trade ministry in the first half of the 1980s independently stated that most of their colleagues would not be able to give a correct account of the theory of comparative cost. There is a body of economic advisers in this ministry, but their views on trade policy were frequently ignored or overruled. In the second half of the 1980s and early 1990s, there have been signs of a more liberal approach to trade policy among officials, again in parallel with the evolution of attitudes among ministers.

Among politicians, views on trade policy have varied widely within the two major political parties as much as between them. In the Labour Party, an interventionist approach to economic policy can readily lead to support for protection. This tendency is reinforced by the close association between the Labour Party and the trade unions, allowing pressure from unions in industries affected by strong competition from imports. For the Conservative Party, in the words of one commentator:

> the trade question is an awkward one since it brings instinctive nationalism and an intellectual commitment to free markets into opposition with each other, especially for a government like the present [Thatcher] one which is strong on both. The difficulties of British industrial companies involved in international trade have long made observers wonder why the classic answer – protectionism – is not embraced by the political Right; the more so as the Conservatives are traditionally the party of protection (there are moreover a good many [Conservative Members of Parliament]

who have developed strong protectionist views). One explanation is that the interests of industrial capital – rather than that of the [finance sector], or the suburban middle class – are no longer the prime concern of the modern [Conservative] party. Another explanation is that the party has found, in government, a way of reconciling free trade and protection which satisfies its business constituency.[1]

In the 1980s, Conservative ministers, supported by the Confederation of British Industries (CBI), embraced the formula that international trade should be 'free but fair'. Speaking to the House of Commons Industry and Trade Committee while he was Secretary of State for Trade and Industry (1983–5), Norman Tebbit said:

> our general attitudes . . . start from a belief in competition, and domestically we have set out to increase our competitiveness through both privatisation and deregulation. Of course, it would make very little sense for a Government which has scrapped pay and prices and exchange controls as a means of establishing a competitive economy at home, to attempt to restrict competition in international trade. Nor would that be in the interest of the UK since an open trading system is a major benefit to us. . . . Of course, we take a pragmatic approach. We seek to ensure that trade is fair as well as free (and to get countries to open to us) . . .[2]

EVOLUTION OF TRADE AND INDUSTRIAL POLICIES

A senior official of the Department of Trade and Industry[3] has suggested that there is no such thing as trade policy, but merely trade measures (or pressure for Community measures) in support of various domestic policies.

At the political level, there was comparatively little debate about free trade *versus* protection in the early post-war years. The United Kingdom was in fact protected against the United States, the strongest industrial power, by exchange controls. The leading controversy over trade policy was whether to try to preserve the system of Commonwealth preferences or to rely on a multilateral, non-discriminatory trading system as envisaged by the GATT. It was recognised that the United Kingdom was highly dependent on imports of primary products and so had a pressing interest in the openness of external markets for its exports. Harold Wilson, as President of the Board of Trade in the Labour Government of 1945–51, is quoted as saying:

> We want to remove import restrictions imposed for balance of payments reasons. We want to see import restrictions which are imposed for less respectable reasons, such as protection of home industries, banned as an instrument of national policy.[4]

There was little public dissent from this approach until the mid-1970s.[5]

Despite the differences in the philosophy of the Conservative and Labour parties, there has often been rather little difference between them in their willingness to provide protection or subsidies to particular industries. It was, for example, a Conservative government which adopted the Cotton Industry Act of 1959, designed to promote rationalisation of the industry. This was accompanied by agreements between the United Kingdom cotton industry and the industries of Hong Kong, India and Pakistan on 'voluntary limitations' of exports to the United Kingdom of cotton fabrics and made-up garments. Protection of the textile industry was subsequently continued and increased by both Conservative and Labour governments. The Macmillan Government also set up, in 1961, the tripartite, corporatist apparatus of the National Economic Development Council.

In 1964, the Labour Government headed by Harold Wilson proposed the use of state support and pressure to promote competitive adaptation of private industry.[6] Responsibility for industry was transferred from the Board of Trade to the new Ministry of Technology. The Department of Economic Affairs (DEA) was set up with responsibilities for general economic planning, sectoral planning, regional policy and wage and price policy. The DEA, however, because it had insufficient financial resources, had little leverage to influence corporate or sectoral strategy.[7] A financial arm to government economic policy was provided by the establishment of the Industrial Reorganisation Corporation in 1966 and the Industry Expansion Act of 1968 which enable the Minister of Technology to make grants or loans to strengthen particular firms.

There was a temporary discontinuity in policy when the Conservative Government took office in 1970, with Edward Heath as Prime Minister. There was, for a time, a deliberate policy of disengagement of government from industrial affairs and of allowing ailing firms to go under. Two major industrial crises, in a fairly short space of time, however, meant that the political costs of standing aside became too great. The Industry Act of 1972 gave the Secretary of State for Industry sweeping powers to give financial assistance to industries – powers which were sufficient to meet the needs of the interventionist Labour Government which came to power in 1974.

A cross-current during this period was the opposition of the left wing of the Labour Party to membership of the Community. When he was President of the Board of Trade from 1974 to 1976, Peter Shore actively explored the possibilities of reviving Commonwealth preferences as an alternative to remaining in the Community. By this time, however, prime reliance on the Commonwealth link was no longer a feasible alternative – even if, indeed, it would have been at any time after World War II.

Increased Protectionism

In the mid-1970s, increased economic strains came from two sources. The first was increasing pressure on manufacturing industry, resulting from the reduction of rates of import duty and the emergence of new international competition, notably from East Asia. The second was the oil price increases of 1973–4.

The first major crack in the consensus favouring liberal trade policies occurred in 1975 when the Trades Union Congress (TUC) pressed for the introduction of selective import controls, including a 20 per cent reduction of imports of textiles, clothing and footwear. When the government did not respond, the Economic Committee of the TUC produced a memorandum arguing that the government should 'fundamentally modify the free trade philosophy on trade and follow a co-ordinated trade and industry policy designed to prevent the further erosion of the UK manufacturing industry base'.[8]

By the time of the Labour Party's annual conference in 1976, import policy was a major issue. Major sections of manufacturing industry – for instance in textiles, footwear, shipbuilding and consumer electronics – were in serious difficulty. The *Financial Times* added to the list 'heavy electrical machinery (mainly the turbine generator and boilermaker industries), paper and board, and, to some extent, the machine tool and constructional steel industries. They virtually declare themselves to be on their uppers'.[9] Moreover, the country was experiencing a balance-of-payments crisis, which necessitated the negotiation, shortly afterwards, of a standby credit from the International Monetary Fund (IMF). In the words of Edmund Dell, Secretary of State for Trade from 1976 to 1978, there was a feeling of being 'under siege'.[10] Influential figures on the left of the government and the Labour Party pressed strongly for import controls, not only to protect particular industries in difficulties, but also in the attempt to permit expansionary internal policies free of the balance-of-payments constraint. This last line was supported by a series of papers, starting in February 1975, from the Cambridge Economic Policy Group (CEPG). For some, the inconsistency with membership of the European Community was an added attraction. (The transitional period of UK membership was due to run to the end of 1977.)

A policy of general or widespread import controls was strongly opposed by both Mr Dell and the Chancellor of the Exchequer, Denis Healey. Mr Dell said that the government would continue its policy of eschewing general import controls. He pointed out that certain temporary and selective import controls were already in force. A strategy of general import controls would isolate the United Kingdom from the world's trading community, and it did not seem to him to go to the root of the problem.[11] Mr Healey, no doubt concerned at the reactions of the IMF, as well as of the United States and other major trading countries whose support for a standby credit would be needed, was particularly outspoken in his speech to the 1976 Party Conference: 'Now, I'll tell you, comrades, the probability is that that would be a recipe for world trade war and a return to the conditions of the 30s.' Moreover: 'General import controls mean an immediate increase in the cost of living, an immediate fall in the standard of living, an immediate increase in unemployment, and immediate problems throughout our economy.' The consequence would be to bring in a Conservative Government.[12] James Callaghan, now Prime Minister, was by no means averse to protection but was well aware that foreign reactions would be strongly hostile.

In October 1976, the Confederation of British Industry (CBI) and the TUC produced a joint memorandum urging action to curb imports of television sets and components, cutlery, motor cars and paper and board. It criticised the Multifibre Arrangement as inadequate and the Community as being too slow in taking advantage of it.[13] The Prime Minister was reported as welcoming the memorandum. The Secretary of State for Trade, however, ruled out widespread import curbs, although in the House of Commons he emphasised that he was prepared to take action in specific cases. The anti-dumping unit in the Department of Trade was being strengthened; and when the Commission took over responsibility for anti-dumping measures on behalf of the United Kingdom producers in 1977, the Department of Trade would retain the necessary capacity to advise the Commission and assist British businesses in bringing cases. While successfully staving off general and widespread import controls, Mr Dell, in accordance with his avowed mercantilism, was by no means averse to granting protection or condoning inter-industry restraint agreements in particular cases.

There was, in fact, less agreement between the TUC and the CBI and, indeed, within the CBI than might have appeared from the joint memorandum. The General Secretary of the TUC was quoted as saying that he would have liked the paper to go much further, while the CBI emphasised the limited scope of its support for import constraints: action must be acceptable to international opinion and rules.[14] The CBI's annual report of 1976, *The Road to Recovery*, rejected the idea of a siege economy. On the other hand, a report by the CBI Europe Committee, while recommending maintenance of liberal policies in external relations, advocated measures to safeguard the Community's own interests, and vigorous action in cases of unfair trading by third countries.[15]

It was against this background that the British authorities took various protective measures. In 1976, while restricting imports of television sets from South Korea and Taiwan, Mr Dell encouraged representatives of the consumer electronics industry to negotiate voluntary restraint agreements.[16] Voluntary restraint agreements were also negotiated at various times with Japanese manufacturers of cars, ball bearings, special steels and pottery. In 1977 Mr Dell and British officials pressed for tighter restrictions under the Multifibre Arrangement.

Conservative Governments of the 1980s

The arrival of the Conservative Government under Margaret Thatcher in 1979 at first brought more change in rhetoric than in actual industrial or trade policies. Sir Keith Joseph, as Secretary of State for Industry, continued to pay out large sums in industrial subsidies, mostly to sectors in difficulty. There was no appreciable change in trade policy. A senior government economist remarked that the government did not appear to understand the logic of its own avowed policies.

There was a greater change of direction in the second Thatcher administration, from mid-1983, and more particularly in industrial policy. The budgetary plans called for a decrease of subsidies to industry and the aim was to concentrate on aid to high-technology activities. In trade policy the idea was floated in the House of Commons that protection of textiles and clothing might be negotiated away, to some extent, in exchange for reduction of protection by developing countries. In the debate of February 1986, however, the Minister for Trade twice asserted: ' . . . I have no intention of getting rid of the arrangement until I am satisfied that the safeguards that it provides are no longer needed.'[17] In the event the government did not hold out against the Commission's proposals for a continued restrictive regime.

There was nevertheless an increased concern in the Thatcher Government to assess the efficiency of government policies and to consider their effects on consumers. Peter Rees, while Minister for Trade (1981–3) successfully supported the production of a report on the cost to the United Kingdom of the Multifibre Arrangement.[18] On the other hand, he was unsuccessful when he advocated the establishment of a public body to hear all parties who would be affected by a proposed protective measure. This proposal was turned down by a committee of ministers on grounds of cost and of a general resistance to setting up new governmental or quasi-governmental bodies. Nevertheless, ministers have sought views in a more informal framework from consumer and importer interests as well as from producers.

INSTITUTIONAL FRAMEWORK

In the United Kingdom, two constitutional principles are of central importance: the collective responsibility of ministers for the actions of the government and the answerability of ministers to Parliament.

When a government has a substantial overall majority in the House of Commons, the main limitation on its room for manoeuvre is the risk of losing power at the next election. Unless there is strong and widespread objection in the party, the government can be sure of getting legislation onto the statute book. It holds over its Members of Parliament the threat that a defeat in the House could well lead to a general election, which would mean trouble, expense and the possibility of being defeated. Nevertheless, ministers are more sensitive to reactions in the House of Commons than this might suggest. Any minister who stirs up too many antagonisms may become a liability in the eyes of the Prime Minister and he could be dismissed from his office; this in turn would prejudice his future political career. (By contrast to the situation in France, British ministers must be members of Parliament – most of them being members of the directly-elected House of Commons.) By extension, Ministers are highly sensitive to views expressed in the national press and television.

This insistence on ministers and Parliament might appear unduly to play down the role of officials. A British member of the European Parliament has said that, in order to bring about a change of policy in the United Kingdom, the first requirement is to secure the support of 'the Establishment' (in other words, officials): even with this support, the policy might still founder on the opposition of ministers, but without it, it would certainly fail. How true is this (not untypical) view of the behind-the-scenes power of senior officials?

In the United Kingdom, the civil service has been a body of career officials, available to serve whatever government may be elected to office. Since the mid-nineteenth century, there has been no practice of political appointments to senior posts, as in France and the United States. There have not been 'political civil servants' in the high-level posts, expressly selected by ministers, as in Germany.[19] Ministers have brought in a certain number of personal advisers who are outside the civil service hierarchy – more in some governments than in others. Career officials have, however, been the main source of information, analysis and advice.

In their relationship with ministers, officials clearly have certain major strengths. Ministers are comparatively few and transitory; there are many officials and they are organised and (by comparison) entrenched.[20] There is a strong working principle in the British civil service that the decision-making capacity of ministers is finite and that consequently there should be a maximum effort to reach agreement on matters of policy at official level. Some ministers have complained that they were not sufficiently advised on possible alternative courses of action, or that official advice to them was effectively controlled by a very few senior officials.

Nevertheless, there are various ways in which ministers can diversify their sources of advice if they make sufficient effort to do so. They may employ personal advisers to act as additional eyes and ears. In many ways, ministers know more about the world than their officials, through constant visits to the areas (constituencies) they represent, through contacts with other Members of Parliament, through representations from interest groups and so on. Ministers concerned with Community matters attend the relevant Council meetings and so, like their senior officials, gain first-hand knowledge of attitudes and possibilities.

Officials, for their part, might attempt to use a network of informal contacts to block courses of action which they consider undesirable; but they can only do this if they can rely on sufficient support at Cabinet level.[21] In the last resort, ministers have the whip-hand through their constitutional position and their (collective) control over the budget and the organisation and staffing of the civil service. Moreover, officials have to be constantly aware of the answerability of ministers to Parliament for all things done under their authority. One consequence of this is that both ministers and senior officials tend to be involved down to matters of quite small detail. In sum, the relationship between ministers and officials in the United Kingdom is complex and subtle.

Inter-ministerial Consultation

As a consequence of the constitutional doctrine of the collective responsibility of ministers, there is an extensive framework of inter-ministerial consultation. Consequently, depending on the allocation of subjects between ministers, a wide range of different points of view may be brought to bear on questions of policy.

Important policy issues are discussed in Cabinet or, for more specialised subjects, in Cabinet committees made up of the ministers with departmental interest in the subject matter. In matters of trade and industrial policies, these will include ministers of the Departments of Trade and Industry (when these are separate), from the Treasury and the Foreign and Commonwealth Office and from other ministries with a legitimate interest. Committees at ministerial level are supported by committees of officials, which clear the papers to go to the ministerial committee.[22] Thus, while the Department of Trade (and Industry) initiates papers on matters of trade policy, other ministries have the opportunity to try to influence policy. As noted above, there is a strong pressure to reach agreement on a single course of action to be proposed to ministers. The convention is, however, that any ministry that insists on stating a conflicting opinion may do so, though the effort is made to set out the dissent in agreed language. After all, officials in the dissenting ministry may be expressing a strongly-held view of their minister, which he will state in any case in the ministerial meeting, or can brief their minister to state the dissenting departmental view.

A ministry which is not consulted, when it considers that it has a legitimate interest, has ways of making its displeasure felt. A common device – somewhat less formal than a letter from one minister to another, copied to other ministers concerned – is a letter at private secretary level. (The private secretary is an official in charge of the minister's private office; he has the task of ensuring the minister gets what he needs to do his job effectively and that the minister's views are duly conveyed to others.)

When the Conservative Government came to power in 1979, a general dislike of excessive bureaucracy led it to decree a drastic reduction of the number of Cabinet and other inter-ministerial committees. Nevertheless, several ministers and ministries have a legitimate interest in a number of policy matters – and certainly in economic policy questions – and it would be unduly cumbrous to handle all these questions by informal arrangements. A general impression suggests that there are as many inter-ministerial committees now, of one kind or another, as under previous governments.

A weakness in the British governmental system is the absence of any unit with overall responsibility for economic policy. The Treasury is limited in performing this function below the macro level, because the prime responsibility for matters of micro-economic policy lies with other ministries – the Department(s) of Trade and Industry, the Department of Energy, the Ministry of Agriculture, Fisheries and Food. The Department of Economic Affairs was unsuccessful; it was wound up in 1969. There has been nothing like the German Economics Ministry, with the general policy role of its Economic Policy Department. The Central Policy Review Staff in the Cabinet Office (set up by Prime Minister Edward Heath in 1971 and disbanded by Mrs Thatcher in 1983) was only able to perform this role in limited degree – in part because of its limited resources and in part because it was not in a major ministry with executive power.[23] The system of checks and balances through inter-ministerial committees has worked up to a point; but the organisation of the government machine leads to a tendency to focus attention on the problems of particular industries, without weighing up the implications of policy for the economy as a whole.[24]

The analysis of policy proposals in a broad framework might, in principle, be carried out by economic advisers in the ministries concerned. The Departments of Trade and Industry, when they were still separate, nominally shared a group of economic advisers. In practice, however, some economists worked for one department and some for the other (and there were some fears that economists might pass on information which the other department was not supposed to know). As in other British government departments (except the Overseas Development Administration and, *de facto*, the Treasury), the economists in Trade and Industry are advisers. That is to say, their advice is asked as and when it is wanted. When economists have no automatic right to be consulted on matters with substantial economic content, there is the constant danger that they will not be kept adequately informed, and it is therefore possible for them to be discredited by their ignorance.

The problems of a lack of broadly-based analysis are compounded by the 'tyranny of the in-tray'. The constitutional rule of the answerability of ministers to Parliament, in small matters as well as large, makes for a considerable focus on detail by ministers and senior officials. The sheer mass of work can tend to crowd out thought on the general direction of policy. In the words of one ex-official of the Department of Trade, 'there was never time to think'. Parties out of power think what they could do with power if they had it. In power, they tend to be more than fully occupied reacting to events as they arise. The result can easily be *ad hoc* decisions, difficult to defend in terms of any coherent view of the aims of policy and of the overall effects of the chosen measures.

Attitudes of Officials to Trade Policy

Officials in different parts of the government machine bring different attitudes to bear on trade policy. It has been noted that, in the earlier post-war years, officials in the trade ministry had a generally liberal orientation and were committed to the principles of the GATT. From the early 1970s, there was an increasing strand of 'pragmatism', and officials were prepared to envisage protection as a reaction to current problems. To some extent, the change can be identified with particular personalities; but this raises the question of whether the presence of certain individuals had a marked effect on policy, or whether the 'pragmatists' were placed in a position of influence because there were widespread pressures for a more protectionist approach. Latterly, there seems to have been some resurgence of the older liberal tradition among officials dealing with trade policy.

Officials dealing with industrial questions provide a natural target for lobbying by producer interests, and these officials may come to identify with the interests of industries seeking protection.

Officials in the Treasury (influenced by economic theory and concern for international economic cooperation) and in the Foreign and Commonwealth Office (concerned to avoid international frictions and impressed by the dangers of retaliatory trade measures by the United States and others), have tended to give such support as they could, through the machinery of inter-ministerial coordination, to the liberal trade strand in the thinking of the Department of Trade.

POLITICAL PRESSURES ON POLICY-MAKERS

Both politicians and officials are aware of the influence of electoral considerations on trade policy. This has been shown particularly clearly by the case of textiles. The system of single-member constituencies, won by the candidate securing the greatest number of votes cast in a single-stage election, leads to the existence of a number of marginal constituencies, where the outcome may determine which party forms the next government. Writing of the situation of the United Kingdom cotton industry in 1966, Sir Arthur Knight said ' . . . Lancashire included a number of marginal constituencies, so that its troubles engaged the interest of politicians especially at times when the political balance was unstable.'[25] Joel Barnett, then a Member of Parliament from Lancashire and Chief Secretary to the Treasury, has recalled how, during the 1977 MFA renegotiation, ' . . . I had made the Prime Minister fully aware, not only of the problems of the industry, but also of the number of marginal seats in Lancashire'.[26] It appears unlikely that the Prime Minister was in need of such warning. Even though the numbers employed in the textile and clothing industries have progressively declined, the political parties have appeared to consider that they would lose more in electoral terms by antagonising the industry than by continuing to protect it at the expense of the remainder of the community. For example, the election manifesto of the Conservative Party in 1979 specifically stated: 'We fully support the renegotiated Multifibre Arrangement for textiles and will insist that it is monitored effectively and speedily.' Questioned on this passage, which might appear to run counter to the generally liberal market approach of the Conservative Party under Mrs Thatcher, a very senior member of the Party confirmed that the passage was inspired by the desire to win votes in textile constituencies. The manifesto before the election of 1983 was less specific; there was no doubt a more general desire to retain the support of manufacturing interests. It said:

> Together with the Community, we are . . . playing a leading part in preserving an open world trading system, while safeguarding our most vulnerable industries.

On the other hand it said:

> We have no intention of becoming a dumping ground for the goods of other nations. We shall continue to challenge other nations' unfair barriers, whether in the shape of tariffs or trading practices.

While the power of the government is strong in relation to Parliament, governments are sensitive to parliamentary opinion, which is by no means without influence. It is symptomatic that the House of Commons debated the future of the Multifibre Arrangement on 9 May 1985 and again on 13 February 1986 (the second debate being 'in response to requests from Honourable Members on both sides of the House'). Such debates are without parallel in Germany and France. Ministers and, consequently, senior officials tend to take notice of pressure groups largely in proportion as their views are reflected in the House of Commons. In addition to the opportunities provided by debates, members of the House of Commons make extensive use of Parliamentary questions to put pressure on the Government.

It is difficult to form a judgement on the effectiveness of trade associations, trade unions and other producer pressure groups in influencing policy; and on what makes one group more effective than another. There is a tendency among ministers and officials to play down the influence of producer groups. Ministers and officials spend a good deal of time conferring with such groups, but this may be to a considerable extent an effort to pacify potential discontent. Their effectiveness, however, tends to depend on the number and strategic importance of votes to be won by meeting their wishes. The case of Lancashire textiles has been a particularly striking example.

At the same time, it is said that (as in France) a group is more effective to the extent that it can make its case in policy-oriented form, readily usable by officials. Groups are ineffective when they are not able to make firm policy requests because they represent divergent interests. Some industries, such as textiles and clothing, steel and cars (manufacturing and trading), lobby heavily through Community-level associations in Brussels, as well as domestically. Some consider that lobbying the European Parliament is a useful reinforcement to lobbying the Commission.

The main channels of influence in the United Kingdom are pluralist rather than corporatist. There were the makings of a corporatist approach when, in 1961, the National Economic Development Council was established. This Council brought together representatives of the government, the Confederation of British Industry (CBI) and the Trades Union Congress (TUC). It was rare, however, that the three pulled in the same direction at the same time.[27] Moreover, both the CBI and the TUC are 'encompassing' organisations, covering broad spans of interests which often conflict. As Lord Watkinson (President of the CBI in 1976–7) wrote: 'it is surprising . . . that the CBI actually represents anything'.[28]

In addition to the Council, there were a number of tripartite sectoral committees – the Economic Development Committees (formerly called Sector Working Parties). When it came to power in 1979, the new Conservative government saw potential utility in the Council, but was sceptical about the sectoral committees. These were defended by both the CBI and the TUC, however, and in time Sir Geoffrey Howe (as Chancellor of the Exchequer and *ex officio* chairman of the Council) came to accept their value in bringing together management, labour and officials to form a common view of the problems of particular sectors and the means of resolving them. The encompassing organisations because of their heterogeneous memberships, however, experienced difficulties in pursuing their ends and sectional interest groups commonly concentrated their efforts on their own individual campaigns. The National Economic Development Council was wound up by the re-elected Conservative Government in 1992.

COORDINATION

The complex of inter-ministerial meetings, correspondence and contacts noted above operates to produce an agreed and known national view. There is not the pressure that exists in Germany or Japan, for example, for all interested ministries to be represented in international meetings to keep an eye on the others.

In addition to the general arrangements for consultation and coordination, however, there is a ministerial committee which deals specifically with Community questions. This is serviced by a special unit in the Cabinet Office, headed by a senior official. The United Kingdom member of the Committee of Permanent Representatives (COREPER) normally comes to London once a week to discuss current business in a committee at the level of officials. Specialist questions, such as trade measures, are normally prepared in the first instance by subject committees. For trade matters, a senior official of the Department of Trade chairs the committee at official-level. There is thus an intimate link between inter-ministerial coordination and the national representation on the Article 113 Committee.

Normally for any major international negotiation, at least two papers will go to the ministerial committee from the official-level committee. The first, at an early stage, is a general preview of the issues likely to arise, with proposals for the general line to be taken by the national representatives. The second paper will be produced when it becomes necessary to make final decisions on the national position. There may be more progress reports or requests for instructions along the way, supplemented by more informal contacts. The minutes of the ministerial meeting, produced by the Cabinet Office, then provide the instructions for the national delegation.

SUMMARY

In the mid-1970s, under pressure of widespread industrial problems and a balance-of-payments crisis, liberal trade policies gave way to a more protectionist approach. A major restraint on the protectionist tendencies of the Labour government in power at the time – tendencies augmented by pressure from trade unions in beleaguered industries – was nevertheless fear of adverse international repercussions. While a major part of the Labour Party favours interventionist economic policies, the Conservatives as a party are more ambivalent. The Conservative Government elected in 1979 professed liberal economic principles, but it was only in the second half of the 1980s that these showed any significant signs of influencing trade policy.

Electoral considerations have been a major influence on British trade policy. Also, while a government with a substantial majority is in a strong position *vis-à-vis* Parliament, ministers tend to be sensitive to the views on trade policy of members of the House of Commons.

The channels of pressure on the government are pluralist rather than corporatist. Interest groups tend to be influential in proportion to the number of electoral votes at stake, though conformity with existing purposes of the government and presentation of arguments in forms readily usable by officials are also an aid to effectiveness.

The constitutional doctrine of the collective responsibility of ministers leads to extensive consultation between ministers and ministries with legitimate interests in any item of business. This, with the formal machinery for coordination of Community business, normally ensures that British government representatives in Community bodies are briefed to take a line reflecting broad agreement or compromise.

In the next chapter, consideration will be given to the question of how policy is made in the Community as a whole.

9 How Decisions Are Made

Before going on to review the interests, pressures and ideas that have shaped Community trade policy, it is necessary to examine who has been more important, and who less, in the formation of policy. It has been seen in Chapter 4 that different commentators have given different interpretations of the locus of decision-making and of the distribution of power, both at the Community and at the national levels.

The answer at Community level might appear obvious: that the decisions are made by ministers from the member governments meeting in the Council (in its various incarnations). The Commission also has a certain influence through its powers of initiative and its role as negotiator on behalf of the Community as a whole with countries in the rest of the world.

As has been seen, however, some analysts have suggested that Community policies are framed by processes which by-pass considered, collective decision-making at the level of the various national governments ('neo-functionalism' and 'transnationalism', with the 'élite network' view emphasising the importance of strategically-placed individuals).

Interpretation in terms of inter-governmental negotiations is examined in the first section of this chapter by considering the relationship between the member governments and the Commission. This is followed by a discussion of the degree of latitude enjoyed by individuals, those in the Commission as well as ministers and officials of member governments, in transacting Community business. Finally, there is a discussion of how negotiations between the member governments are conducted in the Community.

MEMBER GOVERNMENTS AND THE COMMISSION

A general conclusion from this study is that governments, at least of the larger countries of the Community, do all in their power to keep control of trade policy. They have been reluctant to concede Community competence (that is to say, powers of the Commission to take initiatives and to act for the Community as a whole) where this is not clearly specified by the founding treaties; and they have taken full advantage of the provision of Article 113 of the Treaty of Rome which lays down that the Commission shall conduct trade negotiations 'within the framework of such directives as the Council may issue to it'. (While the preceding chapters have examined how government positions on matters of trade policy are determined in three of the largest countries of the Community, another point which remains to be considered is the strength of the feed-back from negotiations at community level into national policies.)

The issue of Community competence is illustrated in the matter of restrictions on imports of endangered species. The Commission argues that the determining factor is the nature of the policy instrument, so that any import control is a matter of trade policy and hence within Community competence. The Council has maintained that the determining factor is the purpose of the measure: this is a matter of ecological and not of commercial policy, and so comes within the ambit of national competence.[1] Of greater importance is the issue of Community competence in negotiations on trade in services in the Uruguay Round of multilateral trade negotiations. Several of the member countries maintained that trade in services was outside the scope of Community competence although they accepted *de facto* that Commission representatives would do the negotiating.

When the Commission undertakes trade negotiations, this is normally within the framework of directives from the Council, and the local embodiment of the Article 113 Committee may be on hand to give 'advice'. Trade ministers from Community countries themselves attended the meeting of the GATT which launched the Uruguay Round and two subsequent meetings of the GATT Trade Negotiations Committee in 1988 and 1990.

Limitations on the latitude allowed to the Commission were strikingly illustrated during the negotiations for the first extension of the Multifibre Arrangement. In July 1977, the French Foreign Minister protested to Commissioner Haferkamp that the Commission had deviated from the negotiating directives received from the Council.[2] It is difficult to see that the French Government had cause for complaint, given the vigour with which the Commission representatives were negotiating for a restrictive agreement. It is possible to imagine how strongly they would have pushed the complaint if there had been an important point of substance.

When in early 1983 Commissioner Davignon, accompanied by Commissioner Haferkamp, discussed restraint agreements in Japan, including an agreement on video cassette recorders, the force of his mandate from the Council was by no means clear. According to *Agence Europe*:

> The German Delegation explained that it is interpreting the mandate given to the Commission as an exploratory mandate which will not give rise to any decisions. On the other hand the French delegation considers that the European Commission should consider itself bound by the Member States' demands. It must negotiate the 'self limitation' in all the sectors where such measures have been called for by France . . .[3]

Before going to Tokyo, Commissioner Davignon consulted national officials by telephone about the desired restraints. Subsequently in the Council the German Economics Minister, Count Lambsdorff, 'expressed certain perplexities as regards the arrangements, which are too similar to "auto limitations" . . .'[4] Given the support for restraint agreements by France, the United Kingdom and others, however, this was simply a statement of principle and did not create a problem for the Commission.

Commission representatives may enjoy a certain freedom of action, in particular when decisions have to be taken under time-pressure in unforeseen circumstances. One senior Commission official (now retired) recalled an occasion when he had had to commit the Community on three or four different matters, in several different places, within the space of a few days. He maintained that, in these circumstances, the Commission can normally obtain retrospective approval by challenging the representatives of member countries to repudiate what has been done in the name of the Community. A minority may make difficulties, but can usually be brought to withdraw their objection if the majority are content.

Moreover, in GATT negotiations for example, a negotiator from the Commission may be in a strong position to argue that the solution which he favours is the best that is negotiable. Speaking of the meeting of the ministerial meeting of the GATT Trade Negotiations Committee of December 1990, the Italian Trade Minister complained that:

> The Commission was practically conducting the negotiations alone. Indeed, 24 frustrated Community Ministers, 12 for trade and 12 for agriculture, were milling around hoping to capture rumors and bits of information on what was occurring . . .

He continued:

> [The ministers'] only actual input was to keep a rigorous watch on the Commission's respect for the negotiation's mandate. The Commission thought that . . . being alone would provide it with greater flexibility. But the result was quite the opposite.[5]

Ministers in this instance were given what has been somewhat cynically described as 'the mushroom treatment': 'They are kept in the dark, and every so often the door is opened and a bucket of manure thrown over them'. Nevertheless, Signor Ruggiero acknowledges the power of ministers, at least to the extent of being able to insist that the Commission should stick to the mandate agreed by the Council. Whether more active participation of 24 ministers, representing the conflicting interest of agriculture and trade in general, would in fact have led to a desirable increase in flexibility is obviously open to question.

Negotiators from the Commission know that there are limits, beyond which they face real risks of repudiation by the Council. They need a good feel for the boundaries of what is likely to be acceptable to the representatives of member governments in the Council, COREPER or the Article 113 Committee. Moreover, while the powers of initiative in matters of trade policy are vested in the Commission, attitudes and policy positions in the Commission are not formed in isolation, but are influenced by continuous contact with representatives of member governments and interest groups. Commissioners or their officials are in constant contact with representatives of the member governments through Council meetings, the meetings of COREPER and of the Article 113 Committee. Senior officials in DG I reckon that they have at least one telephone conversation with an official of one or other member government in a typical working day. One of the functions of the Commissioners' *cabinets* is to act as their masters' 'political antennae'.

One consequence of the need for the Commission to be sensitive to the views of the member governments is that it tends, in general, to take a little by little, 'incremental' approach to policy-making. Nevertheless, that a Commissioner, and the Commission as a whole, can launch a wide-ranging initiative is shown by the 'white paper' *Completing the Internal Market*, of 1985.[6]

IMPACT OF INDIVIDUALS

The conclusion that trade policy arises largely from dialogue between members of the Commission (Commissioners and officials) and representatives of member governments does not rule out the élite network view that decisions are typically made by small numbers of individuals in key positions. The implication of this view appears to be that these individuals are able to exercise considerable discretion in what they do and say. Alternative interpretations emphasise the constraints on individual freedom of action, the systems of rewards and penalties within which the individuals operate. At a more subtle level, there is the question of the processes of conditioning and 'socialisation' whereby individuals come, almost as a matter of course, to reflect the aims and attitudes of the group, be it a national government, a government ministry or a directorate in the Commission, a private enterprise or a socio-economic class.

The Role of Commissioner Davignon

The question of the influence of the individual and the degree of discretion open to him or her is strikingly illustrated by the case of Commissioner Davignon. During his eight years as a Commissioner and subsequently a Vice-President of the Commission (1977 to the beginning of 1985), he played an important part in shaping not only industrial policies, for which he was directly responsible, but also matters of trade policy. He took a leading role in the formation of the Community position on the extension of the Multifibre Arrangement in 1977. He organised the system of steel production quotas in the Community under the 'Davignon Plan' and took the lead in negotiating the steel 'arrangement' with the United States in 1982. He induced Community producers of artificial fibres to agree on supply restrictions. He was midwife to the Esprit programme of cooperative research between electronic firms. In 1983, he negotiated Japanese voluntary restraint agreements on a number of products.

It is interesting to consider what Commissioner Davignon succeeded in doing, which would not have been done by another commissioner in his place. In this connection, it is notable that voluntary delivery guidelines for individual steel producers were introduced in 1976 by Commissioner Simonet, Count Davignon's predecessor. The movement to invoke the manifest crisis clause of the Treaty of Paris[7] can be attributed to the worsening of the market situation and progressive wearing down of German objections by other interested parties. In the steel negotiations with the United States in 1982, Commissioner Davignon was limited in the amount of restraints of steel exports from the Community to the United States that he could offer in order to secure agreement. As to the Esprit programme, the French government was advocating international cooperation and Community governments were in agreement in looking to electronics as an industry of the future.

It is possible that a less determined, energetic and skilful man than Commissioner Davignon would not have secured the Japanese restraint agreement for video cassette recorders; but, in that case, Community governments and industries would no doubt have secured their own bilateral agreements. Perhaps all that was gained was a slight advance of the principle of the common commercial policy, and that almost more symbolic than real.

On the other hand, had there been a commissioner of strong liberal trade convictions in Commissioner Davignon's place in 1977, it is conceivable that the tightening-up of Community protection under the Multifibre Arrangement might have gone somewhat less far.

Commissioner Davignon's strength lay in his great energy and his ingenuity in devising solutions to perceived problems and negotiating tactics. He operated to a great extent through personal contacts and telephone conversations. He had, in general, a strong feeling for how far he could go without running into insuperable opposition, though on occasions he was obliged to pull back. He tended to rely on the support of members of his *cabinet*, and the officials of the relevant Directorates-General (III and I) were not always fully informed of his activities and intentions. On occasions, as in the Japanese restraint agreement of February 1983 for video cassette recorders, the national authorities had difficulty in finding out what had been agreed.

The activities of Commissioner Davignon might appear to lend support to the 'élite network' model of policy formation in the Community; nevertheless it is clear that the views and interests of industries and of governments significantly limited his freedom of action.

CONSTRAINTS ON NATIONAL REPRESENTATIVES

As has been seen, the freedom of action of the Commission is constrained by the need to secure the agreement of the Council; but policy might still be made by a small élite network of politicians, officials and, possibly, representatives of private interests, from the member countries.

It then has to be asked (i) what determines the positions taken by ministers and officials from the member countries, and (ii) what is the degree of discretion that national representatives are able to exercise. These questions relate to the amount of coordination within the various government machines.

Here, the situation is different in the different member countries. In Germany, the Economics Ministry is in a strong position to keep watch over Commission actions in matters of trade policy for industrial goods. It is difficult to imagine that the Economics Ministry would send someone to the Article 113 Committee who did not reflect the liberal market orthodoxy; liberalism has been the orthodoxy of German ministers attending the Council (except notably in agricultural matters and some questions concerning trade in services). Nevertheless, the independence of ministers, enshrined in the German constitution, may allow some scope to the Commission to play off one ministry against another.

When there have been cross-currents in the German position on trade in manufactures, it has been because ministries other than the Economics Ministry have different dominant concerns – for example, the Foreign Ministry with considerations of Community unity or of *Östpolitik*.

In the United Kingdom, the rules of ministerial responsibility to Parliament and of the collective responsibility of ministers lead to a careful and coordinated watch on all significant matters of Community business. The individual minister or official negotiating in a Community body is under strong pressure to reflect the collective aims and political calculations of the government. For example, the British Secretary of State for Trade found it necessary to check with his Prime Minister before agreeing to the details for the 1977 extension of the Multifibre Arrangement. Obviously, a Secretary of State for Trade with strong views on policy can exert a strong influence. But a minister whose views and actions are uncongenial to the Prime Minister, to the Cabinet at large, or even to a large section of the governing party, is likely to find himself moved to another post or relegated to the back benches. Similarly, a few officials in key positions can exercise a significant influence over policy, especially on matters about which their ministers have no very strong views of their own; but they do so within an extensive system of checks and balances, by which a broad range of interests, considerations and pressures are brought to bear on the formation of policy.

The French government, like the British, has formal arrangements for inter-ministerial coordination on questions arising in the Community. While some observers have expressed doubts about the adequacy of coordination within the French government machine, it has been shown in earlier chapters that there is no reason to suppose that the constraints on the individual, the system of checks and balances, is appreciably less strong in France than in the United Kingdom.

Certainly, there can be no general implication that questions of trade policy are 'low politics', beneath the attention of ministers and even of heads of government. For example, two British Prime Ministers took a close interest in successive negotiations of the Multifibre Arrangement. Indeed, it has been seen that the British system, in particular, obliges ministers to concern themselves with quite small details of policy. As noted above, a French Foreign Minister made a personal intervention during the negotiations for the extension of the Multifibre Arrangement in 1977. Count Lambsdorff, as German Economics Minister from 1977 to 1984, made frequent interventions in matters of Community trade policy.

Similarly, it is hardly possible to distinguish whole categories of trade policy as involving so little discretion that they can be relegated as a matter of course to a 'rules track'. In the Community, even anti-dumping procedures involve the exercise of discretion at various different stages. Some trade ministers take more interest than others in matters of detail, but in general ministers tend to involve themselves to the extent that they see a particular question as politically sensitive.

According to Robin Gray, a former senior official in the British Department of Trade and Industry, with long experience of the Article 113 Committee, it is important that the members of the Committee are:

senior officials who come each month from E.C. capitals and who work daily with their ministers. They travel with them and know their ministers' minds – and sometimes more than that. This means that they have close knowledge of domestic political situations that are always important in international trade negotiations or disputes. And they have a knowledge of the broad limits of what is politically tolerable for the Minister and what is not.[8]

A member of the Committee will typically attend with instructions from his capital, 'unless he is lucky enough, as I sometimes was, to be left with broad indications of desired outcomes'.[9]

Thus the general impression is of individuals operating as cogs in much larger machines. One point which nevertheless emerges strongly is the importance of negotiating skills and the influence which can be exercised by a skilled negotiator who may be able to report to his colleagues and superiors that what he proposes is the best (from the national or departmental point of view) that is obtainable. This is part of the process whereby decision-making at the Community level feeds back into the formation of national positions.

NEGOTIATIONS BETWEEN GOVERNMENTS

Participants in negotiations within the Community commonly stress that a very important aspect is the need to reach agreement. This may appear odd in the light of the much-publicised disagreements – over the Community budget for example. In matters of trade policy, however, there is in principle the requirement laid down by the Treaty of Rome to operate a common commercial policy. When the Commission negotiates on behalf of the Community it needs an agreed position – though this may allow separate national quotas, as in the case of the Multifibre Arrangement.

Apart from the requirements of the common commercial policy, the member governments, in general, regard the Community as valuable for political reasons, but have been aware that it has the vulnerability of a recent construction – an awareness which must have been increased by the controversies over the Maastricht treaty. In trade matters, the member governments value the Community as a powerful bargaining unit, with a weight much greater than that of any of the member countries individually.

There is therefore constant pressure to act in ways which can be presented as contributing to the strength of the Community – as *communautaire* – and the existence of the Community, with its purposes as laid down in the Treaties, its institutions and procedures, has built up a 'habit of cooperation'.[10] This leads on to what has been termed 'the professionalisation of negotiations. Those involved tend to see their task as the efficient reconciliation of the dispute'.[11]

Robin Gray has suggested a number of reasons for the effectiveness of the Article 113 Committee. Not only are the members of the full committee senior officials with a thorough knowledge of what is and what is not acceptable to their governments: there is also considerable continuity of membership. The members come to know, also, what is likely to be acceptable to the other national representatives. The fact that the chairmanship rotates between the member countries tends to make members sympathetic to the desire of the current chairman to secure agreement. Mr Gray also stresses the informality of the committee's methods:

> the habit has grown up of discussing more difficult or sensitive subjects over lunch where it is easier to explain problems frankly or to find a way through them. It must be acknowledged that at lunch members refresh themselves with more than a glass of water and a certain mellowing seems to occur.[12]

Use of Trade-offs over Time

The typical method of negotiation in the Community has been to combine a number of issues, so that each member country has the incentive to make concessions on some points in order to secure gains on others. Before most international negotiations, the various national administrations invest a good deal of effort in thinking which issues it would be advantageous to link, which linkages it is desirable to avoid and how the desired linkages, or avoidance of linkages, can be brought about.

Trade issues in the Community have not lent themselves to this sort of packaging. The French Government made acceptance of a number of internal market directives conditional on the establishment of the New Commercial Policy Instrument; but this appears to have been an exceptional case.

In trade questions, the log-rolling appears typically to have been over time, rather than between different issues at any one time. A government will accept a policy which it knows to be of interest to another government unless its own objections are very strong, hoping to receive similar indulgence in the future when its own interests are involved. Ministers in the Council, and national officials, not uncommonly call on the goodwill of others, taking the opportunity to point out informally to their colleagues or to members of the Commission their particular national problems, the implication being that if they receive help on this issue, they will reciprocate on some other issue in the future. Edmund Dell has suggested, for example, that the help he received from the German authorities in 1977 on the distribution of textile quotas was a gesture of goodwill to a colleague in difficulties.[13]

International negotiators commonly refer to 'political capital', the notion that a government stores up future difficulties for itself if its representatives fight vigorously for a national viewpoint on every item on the agenda. Thus a skilled national negotiator, armed with certain powers of discretion, will commonly give way gracefully on points where the national interest is not strong, with a view to being as intransigent as he considers necessary on points of greater national interest. In general, the Germans appear particularly susceptible to appeals to Community solidarity – often supported in trade matters by the knowledge that they would be outvoted if the matter were put to vote. The French, by contrast, have an established technique of arguing for their position up to the last moment or rather beyond, then making the minimum of concessions necessary to secure agreement and congratulating themselves on their cooperative spirit (a view not always shared by others.)[14] A British diplomat with long Community experience suggested that the British were commonly as tenacious as the French, but that the French were perhaps more inclined to invent artificial difficulties.

Despite the pressures to reach agreement, and the 'habit of cooperation', ministers and officials may still take rigid positions when they see the need or are under strong pressure to do so. It has been seen that the Commission had difficulty in putting restraint agreements with exporters on a common Community basis, even when the negotiations were carried out by the Commission. On the other hand, when in July 1982 the United Kingdom secured approval from the council for bilateral negotiations with the United States over steel, this decision was reversed only four days later and the exclusive mandate to negotiate was returned to the Commission.

SUMMARY

It would appear that the governments of the larger countries of the Community at any rate do all in their power to keep control of trade policy. This severely limits the freedom of action available to Commissioners and officials of the Commission.

There are arrangements, of varying degrees of strength, for interministerial coordination of the handling of Community questions in the three countries which have been considered in detail. Matters of trade policy are often considered at the highest level of government. The Article 113 Committee plays an important part in shaping Community trade policy. It is able to do so in large part because it is made up of officials who know what is acceptable to the governments they represent.

In general, individuals involved in making trade policy – national ministers, Commissioners and officials – operate as cogs in their respective machines, subject to a variety of pressures and constraints. Nevertheless a skilled negotiator, either for a national government or the Commission, may be in a strong position to argue that a certain course of action is the best that is negotiable, but he still needs to be sensitive to what is acceptable to his superiors and colleagues.

There are strong pressures in the Community to reach agreement between conflicting national positions. National representatives may give way on one point in the hope that others will be equally indulgent on a future item of pressing interest to their own authorities. Thus, while the various governments form their own views on matters of Community trade policy, they are influenced by considerations of what is likely to be acceptable to the representatives of other Community countries, but they can fight vigorously when a major interest is involved.

The various pressures and influences operating on ministers and officials involved in making Community trade policy will be con sidered more closely in the next chapter.

10 Interests and Pressures on Policy-Makers

The question was raised in Chapter 1 of the extent to which Community trade policy has been influenced (i) by ideas of the public or national good and of the necessary means to secure the desired ends, and (ii) by the self-interest of politicians, officials, or private parties. In this chapter the interests of politicians and officials are discussed as well as the pressures and constraints to which they are subject. The degree of influence exercised by private interests and pressure groups is also considered.

This chapter is divided into four main sections, which will examine:

(a) the interests of, and influences on, politicians who are concerned with the making of trade policy;
(b) the interests of the officials who advise member country ministers or Commissioners, and the pressures and influences on them;
(c) the influence exercised by private pressure groups; and
(d) the international pressures and the influences arising from the existence and nature of the Community.

These categories are not, of course, water-tight compartments. There are complex interrelationships between the interests of the participants in the policy-making process and the pressures and influences to which they are subjected. It is difficult to assess the relative importance of these various elements and the interrelationships between them. An attempt will nevertheless be made to draw inferences from decisions which have been made over a period of about 15 years and to assess statements made by politicians and others in connection with trade policy.

INTERESTS OF, AND INFLUENCES ON, POLITICIANS

The responses to a mini-survey of a number of ex-ministers and senior officials in the United Kingdom strongly confirmed that the primary interest of politicians is in winning and/or maintaining the support of the electorate. Governing parties wish to remain in office and to build up and retain sufficient support to be able to exercise power effectively. Because of this they are subject to a number of influences.

In general, politicians expect to win more votes by providing favours to producer groups than they lose by imposing costs on consumers. Even when those engaged in a particular form of production come to form a fairly small minority of the population in a certain area, there may be more votes to be gained by providing favours to these producers than to be lost from those who pay the costs (in higher prices of protected goods or in taxes to pay for subsidies). It is a commonplace that economic benefits to particular groups tend to be concentrated and conspicuous and so good for political support, while the costs are widely spread and may be little noticed. The difficulty of raising widespread support for pressure groups in the interests of the consumer has been widely noted in the literature.[1]

In the United Kingdom, importance has been ascribed to 'buying off producer group pressures', although some officials regard this as significant but of secondary importance. It appears that Ministers are reluctant to affront any significant interest group and particularly one which is vocal in the defence of its interests. They will only do so if there is some fairly strong reason of government policy or political calculation (that the importance of the votes lost is outweighed by that of the votes gained or retained). People who have lost what they have come to expect are more aggrieved than those who bear costs (of protection or subsidisation) which they may barely, if at all, apprehend.

Reciprocity and Fairness

In speeches on trade policy in the latter part of the 1980s frequent references were made to the concept of 'fairness'. Even in Germany, there was increasing concern with considerations of fairness in trade relations.

The notion of fairness is indeed embodied in the GATT, which allows protection against 'unfair' competition in the form of dumped and subsidised goods. Economists – at any rate those of the liberal trade persuasion – look askance at this concept of fairness. They argue that the total welfare of a country can be increased by taking cheap imports, irrespective of the reasons for their cheapness (unless there is a threat of monopoly power which will subsequently be used to the disadvantage of the importing country). Ministers and officials, on the other hand, maintain that it is necessary to convince important producer groups that the government (or the Community) is taking steps against unfair international competition, in order to maintain the necessary support for a substantial degree of openness in international trade.

The concept of fairness is notoriously elastic. Japanese surpluses on current account, or even bilateral surpluses with the Community, may be regarded as evidence of unfairness. Alleged 'targeting' of exports may be branded as unfair. Competition on the basis of low labour costs is commonly denounced as unfair, especially by those who are directly hurt by it. In terms of political support, governments may be tempted to pay heed to complaints of unfair foreign competition. They also see the need, however, to put into the balance considerations of gains from trade and the maintenance of some kind of viable international trading system. Thus they may emphasise 'fair trade' in speeches, while accepting that certain foreign practices have to be, or even should be, accepted.

Reciprocity, on the other hand, is built into the GATT and has become something of a reflex in international trade negotiations. For example, in a paper by the Commission on the implications for external trading relations of the completion of the Community's internal market it is stated that:

> the Community's aim is to strengthen the multinational system in accordance with the concept of balance of mutual benefits and reciprocity. These are two internationally accepted principles of trade policy in GATT and in the OECD. The experience of the GATT shows that in those multilateral negotiations designed to liberalize market access, progress is achieved because all the participants exchange 'concessions' so everyone achieves a balance of advantages from the negotiations.[2]

The motivation of the desire for reciprocity is nevertheless somewhat ambiguous. On the one hand, it may spring from considerations of national economic welfare: it may be thought that other countries' protection is sufficiently economically damaging for it to be worth while retaining protection at home as a bargaining counter. (This feeling is so much the stronger if domestic protection is seen as costless or even beneficial.) On the other hand, the desire for reciprocity may spring as much or even more from political motives – the desire to show an offset when an advantage to some section of the population is surrendered, even if the offset does not accrue to the same people who lose an advantage. This is one example among many of mixed motivation in trade policy, making it difficult to judge the relative weight of the various motives.

The politicians and officials consulted in the United Kingdom attributed a fair degree of importance to the appearance of striking a good bargain for the country. Irrespective of any form of economic calculation, trade negotiators and politicians may wish to be seen to strike a hard bargain. A British trade negotiator admitted the temptation to score points, for the joy of winning, and speculated that certain ministerial demands for more protection might have been motivated by pure combativeness.

INTERESTS OF, AND INFLUENCES ON, OFFICIALS

It has been suggested that 'Every official is significantly motivated by his own self-interest even when acting in a purely official capacity'.[3] Nevertheless, it is acknowledged that an official's self-interest may include pride in good work and a desire to serve the public interest; officials are also influenced by the environment in which they work.

An official is paid to do a particular job. The position he takes on an issue of policy will depend to a not inconsiderable extent on his place in the organigram. The civil service in the United Kingdom, for example, works to a great extent through a system of adversary proceedings – between different ministries, with their different viewpoints, and between different divisions within ministries. Officials will have their own views on policy, but to a great extent they have to perform their allotted roles (and may significantly change the positions they take on matters of policy if they are posted from one part of the bureaucracy to another).

Departmental Interests

In deciding positions on policy or tactics within a ministry or division in a ministry, there are times when argument is acceptable or is even encouraged. There are other times when ministers and senior officials share agreed views on what should be done and regard dissenting opinions as a unacceptable waste of valuable time. Conventional wisdoms can spring up and become entrenched. The position of senior officials is justified by their wisdom. 'Wisdom' can consist in uttering views congenial to influential listeners. There is then pressure to consider (consciously or subconsciously) what approach is likely to be considered wise. Dissent can carry penalties, in loss of position or at least of influence. There are strong pressures on individuals to argue only when they believe that they have a reasonably good chance of success or when they regard the issue as so important that it would be a dereliction of duty to keep silent. Here, indeed, there is a range of individual behaviour from the sycophants to the mavericks; but the mavericks tend to be ignored or pushed aside as 'unsound'.

There are, of course, some relatively strong influences on officials who are dealing with industrial questions and these influences may also interact with the departmental interests. First, there is the desire to build up an influential client group, which will support the continued existence and operational importance of the unit. Second, to be seen to be performing their functions effectively, officials need information, for which they are dependent on people in the industries themselves. In order to secure information, they have to be able to hold out the hope of benefits in return. Third, continued contact with people in an industry naturally disposes them to see the world from the industry's viewpoint.

The bias in policy-making towards various industrial interests then depends on the strength of countervailing forces in the system. Officials in divisions dealing with international trade, whether they are in the same ministry as the industry specialists or in another ministry, will tend to emphasise such matters as the risk that protection and subsidies will provoke retaliation by other countries, the breaking of the rules of the GATT and so on. Foreign ministries everywhere are concerned to promote good relations with other countries, except, in varying degrees, with those countries regarded as hostile. They therefore tend – in so far as they have any effective voice in matters of trade policy – to advocate liberal trade policies as a contribution to amity between nations. In the United Kingdom the Treasury has responsibilities for the general oversight of economic policy, but it has not exercised much influence on trade policy.

However great the degree of inter-ministerial coordination, the ministry with prime responsibility for a subject is always in a position of some strength in relation to other ministries even where these can assert a legitimate interest. Moreover, the industry specialists have an important advantage in their superior knowledge of relevant facts, which may tend to carry weight against arguments based on economic theory or other general considerations.

Activism

Both ministers and officials have an interest in being seen to 'do something'. Although senior officials deny this on the grounds that they have quite enough to do without going out to look for work, nevertheless it is natural to suppose, for example, that the existence of a ministry or department of industry creates pressures for active industrial policies. Officials consider that they are there to solve problems. This has been notably true in France, where senior officials and many ministers have been indoctrinated in interventionist habits of thought in the *grandes écoles*.[4]

The Commissioners and Commission officials, like other politicians and bureaucrats, have strong incentives to be seen to 'do something' in order to defend their positions. They can justify most of their activities in terms of the Commission's role (together with the European Court of Justice) as guardian of the Treaties. Moreover, there is a natural tendency to try to assert a maximalist rather than a minimalist interpretation of this role. Critics of Commissioner Davignon, with his highly active role in matters of industrial and trade policy, maintain that he was actuated more by a desire to build up his own role and that of the Commission than by any systematic, strategic view of economic management. Commissioners and Commission officials, like national politicians and officials, find it desirable to attract the support of grateful clients.

INFLUENCE OF PRIVATE PRESSURE GROUPS

Some reference has been made to the response of ministers and officials to representations on behalf of particular private interests. Pressure groups operate in the Community at both the national and the Community levels. The question then arises of what determines the impact on policy made by the various pressure groups.

In the first place, a pressure group is likely to be successful if there are strong electoral considerations at stake. The number of parliamentary districts (constituencies) in the cotton textile areas of

Lancashire liable to swing at elections to one or other of the major parties has, in the past, had a strong influence on the policy of British governments towards textiles.

Secondly, companies or trade unions may be influential as major contributors to the funds of political parties. In some cases, individuals may secure favours through their particular political contacts. For example, it is said that in Germany a particular individual was able, through personal political influence, to secure the maintenance of high protection on decorated pottery, even though this was contrary to general policy.

Thirdly, a pressure group tends to be particularly influential, in France and no doubt elsewhere, if its efforts correspond with a policy interest of the government, for example the desire to build up high-technology industries. Moreover, given the felt need in the government machine for information on developments in the various industrial sectors, as a basis for policy decisions, the representatives of sectors with specialised, diversified and fast-evolving products may be at an advantage through their monopoly of technical information. It may be in part for this reason that the association of the chemical industries is said to be notably influential in the United Kingdom. The influence of a particular industry tends to be especially strong if it is nationalised or in receipt of substantial subsidies, because then the government can hardly avoid feeling responsible for its success (though a new government may withdraw support).

At the Community level, industry associations can play a certain role in recommending and urging policies – provided that competition between producers in the various Community countries allows agreement on a sufficiently strong and unified view. For the steel producers, EUROFER, set up at the instigation of the Commission to represent the steel producers at Community level, is in a particularly strong position because it is dealing with the Commission which has powers in this sector far exceeding those it possesses in other sectors (except agriculture). But even for steel, what might be termed the strategic decisions are taken by representatives of national governments in the Council.

Commissioner Davignon followed the method of first securing the agreement of industry representatives to a course of action before entering into negotiations with governments. Indeed, witnesses suggested that he virtually extended an open invitation to major industries to bring their problems to the Commission. The combination of an active and resourceful Commissioner and an agreed industry position clearly put strong pressure on governments. Philips, the giant manufacturer of electrical and electronic goods, with head-quarters in the Netherlands, appears to have been particularly suc-cessful in influencing the Community's import policies. At the same time, governments have to take a broad view of their policy aims and of the conditions of political survival, and are by no means helpless against a producer coalition mobilised around the Commission.

Moreover, it appears that national industry associations more often than not consider it important to seek support from their own govern-ments for the policies they wish to see followed in the Community. Indeed some, perhaps most, national industry associations consider lobbying their own government more important than lobbying the Commission.

Interest group representatives are said to be more effective to the extent that they produce material in forms readily usable by the officials (in particular) with whom they deal. It may well be, however, that effective and insistent presentation of the industry's case is not particularly influential. A retired senior official from the Department of Industry in the United Kingdom likened the representations of trade associations to 'the radio going in the kitchen', – in other words, background noise vaguely heard but not particularly attended to. Nevertheless, officials in 'industry' ministries, or divi-sions of ministries, provide a ready focus for lobbying by producer interests. How successful this lobbying is likely to be then depends on the system of checks and balances within the bureaucratic and political machine.

In terms of forming coalitions, political parties tend to look to peak organisations, whether of industries and employers or of trades unions. As Mancur Olson, the eminent sociologist, points out, however, these 'encompassing organisations' are made up of mem-bers with conflicting interests – for example, some who desire protec-tion and others who would regard themselves as harmed by such protection. The peak organisations therefore tend to take broad and balanced views of micro-economic policy. It is, perhaps, partly for this reason that they appear to be rather ineffective in influencing policy.[5]

One point that has emerged so far is that surprisingly little political weight is attached to the commercial or industrial interests which are disadvantaged, through loss of trade or increased prices of inputs, by acts of protection. It appears that, by and large, these interests have not succeeded in making their voices effectively heard. In general, the Commission has left the responsibility of representing consumer and user interests to national governments, although spokesmen for these interests have the right to make representations in Community hearings on anti-dumping and countervailing duties. User interests, often dispersed, tend to be less strongly represented than producer interests. Within bureaucracies, the unit dealing with the producers tends to be in the lead in sectoral matters and this can put the units dealing with users' interests at a disadvantage.

INTERNATIONAL PRESSURES

Many of the pressures and considerations reviewed in the two preceding sections tend in the direction of protection and of domestic industrial support. At the international level, however, there are strong influences towards caution in such policies: (i) fear of retaliation, and (ii) the influence of the GATT.

Fear of Retaliation

Whenever measures of protection (or the use of subsidies) are considered, policy-makers have to take into account the risk of retaliation and emulation by other countries. Such retaliation may be considered as damaging in terms of economic welfare, or erosion of political support, or both.

Fear of retaliation, particularly by the United States, is a strong constraint, or at the least a cautionary influence, on increases in protection. Under the fear of damaging retaliation, Community trade policies are shaped in considerable degree not only by the provisions of the GATT but also by United States trade laws. Statutes enacted by the United States Congress lay down the conditions under which the Administration shall judge imported goods to be dumped; shall judge imports to be subsidised; or may or may not negotiate in the GATT; and so on. Interested parties in the United States can take the Administration to court for non-fulfilment of rights conferred by the legislation. Thus, for the United States, it is domestic legislation that is operative and the provisions of the GATT operate only as they are reflected in this legislation. Given the weight of the United States in international trade, those in the Community who decide and administer trade policy need to be as familiar with United States trade laws as with the rules and procedures of the GATT.

Influence of the GATT

It was seen in Chapter 2 that the Community's attitude to the GATT is decidedly ambivalent. On the one hand, it values the GATT (i) as a forum in which it can put pressure on other countries to abandon practices which reduce the opportunities open to producers in the Community, and (ii) as an instrument for regulating trade relations with the United States. On the other hand, several aspects of Community trade policy are contrary at least to the spirit of the GATT rules.

In the important matter of regulation of trade disputes, the agreed position in the Community is that the function of the GATT is to provide a forum for the settlement of trade disputes by negotiation. Community spokesmen accuse the United States authorities of excessive legalism in their approach, and of 'testing to destruction' the dispute settlement procedures of the GATT. Clearly, there is a desire in the Community not to surrender its freedom of action any more than is necessary to restrain unduly damaging action by others. There is also the fear that the Community may be more effectively restrained than the United States by rulings of the GATT, since the United States Administration may claim that the Congress prevents it from complying. (United States representatives, on their side, have accused the Community's negotiators of sticking too rigidly to the letter of the GATT when it suits them, and of being insufficiently willing to look for compromises.)

PRESSURES WITHIN THE EUROPEAN COMMUNITY

It was concluded in Chapter 9 that a major influence on trade policy stemming from the existence of the Community is the pressure on the member countries to reach agreement.

It has been suggested that the Community is 'about discrimination'. The common external tariff, together with the free circulation of goods (in principle) within the Community, is one of the important features distinguishing the Community from the rest of the world. This might bias the Community in favour of retaining (common) protection against the outside world. In fact, there is no evidence of protection being used simply to increase the distinctiveness of the Community. Indeed, the Community has been prepared to reduce the common external tariff as its contribution to negotiations in the

GATT and to advance the tariff cuts agreed in the Tokyo Round of trade negotiations as its contribution to 'standstill and rollback of protection'. Where protection has been increased in recent years, this can be attributed to other influences and considerations.

The presidency conclusions at the meeting of the European Council in June 1988 affirmed the principle that after 1992 'the internal market should not close in on itself'. This was no doubt designed to reassure the Community's trading partners, not least the United States, and to avoid providing a provocation to, or excuse for, protectionist action by others. The statement goes on to say:

> In conformity with the provisions of GATT, the Community should be open to third countries, and must negotiate with those countries where necessary to ensure access to their markets for Community exports. It will seek to preserve the balance of advantages accorded, while respecting the unity and the identity of the internal market of the Community.

There is thus a strong emphasis on reciprocity and the final phrase of the statement appears designed to satisfy those who hold that, if competition becomes too uncomfortable, external trade policy should be adapted to the priority of completing the common internal market.

SUMMARY

The strongest interest influencing trade policy is the interest of politicians in retaining and increasing electoral support and in winning the next election. Frequently, politicians expect to gain more support by meeting the wishes of producer groups than they will lose by imposing costs (of protection or of financing subsidies) on the rest of the population. This tendency is augmented by the familiar difficulty of organising effective representation of the dispersed consumer interest. It is considered politically important to protect producers against foreign competition which can be plausibly represented as unfair. Insistence on reciprocity in international trade bargaining also appears to be largely motivated by political considerations: the desire to show benefits for some parts of the population even if protection of other parts is reduced.

Officials, like Ministers, have an interest in being seen to 'do something' to justify their positions. This may incline them towards interventionist policies. There is no doubt something in the argument that officials in departments dealing with industrial affairs need information which can only come from the industries themselves; officials therefore have an inducement to hold out the prospect of favours in return. Such officials provide a target for lobbying activities; and in policy discussion they have the advantage of detailed knowledge of the relevant facts.

Producer groups are most effective when they represent votes which may prove critical in certain electoral districts, when their aims correspond with some aspect of government policy (such as the desire to develop high-technology activities), when they are able to provide specialised information desired by the bureaucracy and when they present their case in a form readily usable by officials (probably in that order of importance). Such groups commonly consider it more important to lobby their national government than to make representations to the Commission (though they may of course do both if resources allow, and in particular if they can make common cause with producers in other Community countries). In general, groups representing industrial users of imports seem to have been remarkably ineffective in resisting protection.

While the interests of politicians and of some officials produce a bias in favour of protection and industrial subsidies, this is counterbalanced by fear of the adverse political and economic effects of retaliation or emulation by other countries.

Much in trade policy can no doubt be explained by the play of interests examined in this chapter. This does not, however, preclude significant influences on policy of ideas of the public or national good and of the means required to achieve the desired aims. The influence of ideas will be explored in the next chapter.

11 The Influence of Ideas on Trade Policy in the Community

The previous chapter reviewed various interests and pressures affecting trade policy in the Community. On the one hand, there are a number of private, bureaucratic and political interests which tend in the direction of interventionist economic policies and protection. On the other hand, protection and subsidisation are often discouraged by fears of retaliation by other countries, considered to be damaging economically, politically or both.

Largely missing from this discussion has been the influence of ideas. Governments come into power with more or less agreed policy aims. As a government's term of office progresses, however, ministers are forced to react to events and pressures and as the time for the next election comes inexorably closer, the main concern of governments will be to maintain sufficient support to secure re-election. In any case, ministers and officials find it necessary to justify or explain the policies recommended or implemented in terms of considerations of the public or national good and of the means necessary to achieve the desired ends. Other explanations in terms of desirable ends and necessary means have been suggested by academics and other commentators.

The range of possible explanations of Community trade policy in terms of its economic or social rationale is extensive. In this chapter, such explanations will be grouped under the following heads:

(a) liberal trade theory;
(b) mercantilist arguments of various kinds;
(c) arguments of social welfare relating to loss of income by particular economic or social groups;
(d) arguments related to the economic costs of adjustment and the impact of competition from the newly-industrialising countries and from Japan;
(e) the view that international comparative advantage is now largely man-made and can be favourably influenced by infant industry protection; and

(f) arguments related to balance-of-payments problems and the instability of exchange rates.

Some of these stated justifications or explanations of policy are clearly erroneous, or at least highly suspect. This raises the question whether they are in fact simply manifestations of 'do-it-yourself economics' which will not stand up to rigorous examination,[1] or whether the alleged considerations are in fact simply acts of persuasion or would-be respectable cover for the interests examined in the preceding chapter.

LIBERAL TRADE THEORY

It is convenient to start from liberal trade theory, which concludes that only in certain special cases (often impossible to implement in practice) is protection the first best policy in terms of national economic welfare. This body of theory is coherent and has been put to the test of academic discussion over the years.[2]

While liberal trade theory has been influential, at any rate up to a point, in Germany and in the United Kingdom, it is noticeable that many practitioners of trade policy – ministers and officials in the Commission as in national governments – are quite vehement in rejecting the prescription of unilateral free trade.

It has been seen that since the end of World War II German governments have made a conscious decision to adopt free-market economic policies. This approach was reinforced by economic success and by the need of governments to differentiate themselves both from the Nazi past and from the regime in East Germany; it has been buttressed by various institutional arrangements. Thus the principle of the free-market approach has not been in dispute among the major political parties in the Federal Republic.

In the United Kingdom, also, liberal trade theory has formed a background orthodoxy, though clearly it has often not been the dominant influence. Of British insistence on tightening up protection at the time of the renewal of the Multifibre Arrangement in 1977, a retired senior official said: 'we did it with a bad conscience', but this did not prevent him from fighting vigorously for the protectionist policy desired by his minister. In France, liberal trade theory has made very little impact in the face of more interventionist theories and attitudes (see Chapter 7).

Even in Germany, some would say that the dominant consideration behind trade policy has been interest in exports of manufactures
and consequent dislike of policies which might provoke or encourage
an increase of protection in the United States and other export
markets. It is noticeable that the free trade approach has been
stronger in the Economics Ministry and with its successive ministers,
and in relation to manufacturing industry, than in other parts of the
German government machine and with regard to other sectors of the
economy. Ex-Commissioner Tugendhat has put forward an essentially mercantilist explanation of trade policy in Germany as also in
other countries of the Community:

> Governments . . . take a view on where their overall balance of
> interest lies. If they think their national companies will benefit
> from freer competition they support it, as with the British govern-
> ment and insurance. If they think their own firms will lose out they
> will probably fight a prolonged rearguard action against it, as the
> German government has done in the same case.[3]

MERCANTILISM

The antithesis of liberal trade theory are mercantilist arguments of
various kinds. Edmund Dell was unusual among British Secretaries
of State for Trade in setting out a general exposition of his thinking
on policy, and unusual in describing himself as an avowed mercantilist.

> Mercantilism is an expression of the ordinary human feeling that
> one's own nation must come first. Mercantilism expresses the belief
> that international trade is a kind of war in which it is better to win
> than to lose. You win by having a surplus and you lose by having a
> deficit.[4]

After the great depression of the 1930s, 'the new mercantilism' was
associated with beggar-my-neighbour policies, whereby each country
tried to shift unemployment onto other parts of the world. Dell
emphasised two other considerations in particular: (i) that a country
should not become dependent on imports of essential goods, and (ii)
that it should not become dependent on the goodwill of others in
order to finance current account deficits. 'There are many aspects of
economic strength but the most important is simply this: one should

reduce, not increase, one's dependence on the goodwill of other governments, particularly the need to borrow from them or from international agencies established by them'. He saw a general political aspect: 'Friendship flourishes best when the demands made on it are least'.

It might have been thought that the British government under the premiership of Mrs Thatcher would be more committed to free trade because of its general economic philosophy than appeared in practice. One ex-Secretary of State, when asked what had been the main obstacle to applying his avowed liberal trade principles, replied, 'Margaret [Thatcher] is a nationalist.' Mercantilism has many facets and the general sentiment as defined by Edmund Dell continues to exercise its influence as a branch of 'do-it-yourself economics'.

CONSIDERATIONS OF INCOME DISTRIBUTION

The third explanation, or justification, for particular trade policies adopted by governments is concerned with income distribution. Professor Max Corden, a leading advocate of liberal trade policy, has suggested that a major reason for departures from this prescription is what he terms the 'conservative social welfare function' – the aim that 'any significant absolute reductions in real incomes of any significant section of the community should be avoided'.[5]

Professor Corden suggests various different considerations that might underlie this kind of policy objective. In the first place, there may be the value judgement that it is unfair to allow anyone's real income to be reduced significantly, especially if this is the result of deliberate policy decisions. Such a principle might appear perverse, in that it could lead to measures to protect some people's incomes at the expense of others who are worse off. Nevertheless, it is not implausible that abrupt, unexpected losses of income by particular, identifiable groups in the community are conspicuous and attract sympathy. Moreover, Corden suggests that, if people are averse to taking risks, everyone's welfare is increased if it is known that the government will generally intervene to prevent sudden or large and unexpected income losses. Although Corden does not specifically mention the point, it is an element in the liberal trade prescription that the gainers could compensate the losers, so that everyone could be better off; but if the losers do not expect to be adequately compensated, this argument carries little weight with them.

Another argument put forward in this context is that social peace may be disturbed if some groups become abruptly worse off while others prosper. There is also the related element of political interest – that political stability and the government's hold on power might be threatened.

In Max Corden's view, the conservative social welfare function explains why countries (and the Community) have been interested in 'voluntary' restraint agreements even though they turn the terms of trade (ratio of export prices to import prices) against their own countries and hand windfall profits to the foreign suppliers.[6] Other testimony to the reality of the conservative social welfare function can be found. When he was Secretary of State for Trade in the United Kingdom, Norman Tebbit declared: 'Politics is about perceived justice' as well as economic efficiency. Politicians have to consider 'what is tolerable to voters within a democratic society'.[7] Other evidence is the widespread pressure for redundancy payments to those who lose their jobs, over and above the standard social security benefits. In sum, the idea of the conservative social welfare function would appear to make a certain contribution to the explanation of Community trade policy; but it is only part of the story.

REACTIONS TO EXTERNAL COMPETITION

It has been emphasised, in Chapter 5, that Community trade policy in the period covered by this study was made against the background of recurring periods of recession, persistent high unemployment, and economic pressures for major adjustment and restructuring in the face of technological developments and changing patterns of international competition.

Against this background, various arguments have been advanced in favour of protection of industries in the Community. Protection of or subsidies to particular industries have commonly been justified in terms of 'reducing the costs of adjustment' or 'buying time for adjustment'. Beyond this, there have been more fundamental arguments that competition from countries with socio-economic systems greatly different from those of Western Europe is inherently damaging, and should be countered by protection. In particular, Japan has been seen as posing special problems, justifying protection against Japanese goods as well as pressure on the Japanese to change their trading practices and macro-economic policies.

The Adjustment Problem

Ex-Commissioner Davignon has supported the use of protection in the effort to ease necessary processes of adjustment. In his preface to a book on international trade law, he wrote:

Having been personally involved in the formulation of the Community trade policy during those difficult years, it is my firm belief that protection can never be a proper substitute for adjustment in a world economy characterized by rapid shifts in comparative advantages. However, it is equally true that, in the face of these radical changes, a number of industries need 'breathing space' in order to reorganize themselves at an acceptable social cost. By making transitions smoother, the judicious use of the instruments authorized and controlled by GATT can usefully contribute to adjustment.[8]

At the time of the second extension of the MFA in 1981, the Commission produced a communication to the Council arguing for 'a combined effort by the industry to ensure that production in the Community's textile and clothing sector does not fall below the level of the last few years'.[9] The communication suggested that:

An uncontrolled transfer of the textile and clothing industry [to other parts of the world] *would not be advisable in the current economic situation.* . . . The textile and clothing industry is not only one of the Community's biggest industrial employers; it also employs people with a training which fits them for few alternative jobs. This factor is all the more important when it is realised that the industry is usually sited in places where it is a major employer or where other industrial employers are similarly affected by the economic recession.[10]

This document reveals certain internal contradictions, presumably reflecting differences between the specialists in DG III and, for example, the guardians of competition policy in DG IV. Moreover, the argumentation is not always entirely clear. The intended emphasis may be largely on the social costs of adjustment. This relates to the questions discussed under the heading of the conservative social welfare function. There may also be the thought that, in a period of generally high unemployment and particularly in depressed areas, workers thrown out of their jobs will not find, or will not find at all soon, alternative employment of adequate productive value. Thus it has been argued that by protection it is possible to avoid undesirable losses of productive capacity. This would appear to be the implication of a remark, by a senior official dealing with trade policy in the United Kingdom, that policy needs to take account of the demonstrated limited adaptability of the British economy.

Such arguments readily lead to what might be called the 'bird-in-the-hand' syndrome – the view that it is desirable to prop up existing, uncompetitive activities, because not enough new or expanding activities will rise up to take their place. A related consideration which has been strong in France, and in a varying degree in other Community countries, is the desire to preserve the economic base of particular regions or localities threatened by foreign competition. This may be a matter of vote-counting, or of other aspects of the conservative social welfare function. In addition, it is sometimes argued that migration from depressed areas creates demand for costly new social infrastructure in the areas gaining population.

In times of widespread high unemployment, the 'bird-in-the-hand' reaction can easily appear to be no more than common sense. Recession opens the way to special pleading that industries will become profitable again when economic activity turns up once more, if only they are helped to survive in the meantime. It may also be argued that such help would enable the industries to make the necessary adjustments.

The 'bird-in-the-hand' syndrome tends to be reinforced by the phenomenon of sectoral blinkers, whereby different parts of the administrative machine, concentrating on particular industries, consider only the advantages of particular policies to those industries and ignore the costs imposed on other parts of the economy. This blinkered vision can carry up to the highest policy-making levels, when attention is focused on various industries in crisis at different times – textiles at one time, steel at another and cars at yet another.

In the reactions of policy-makers, there has been a tendency to ignore, or at any rate to play down, the costs and inefficiencies arising from protection, subsidisation and cartelisation, when these are balanced against the supposed economic and social costs of adjustment. All too often, little account has been taken of the important arguments that protection and subsidies distort the market signals which would encourage necessary adjustments and impose costs on other parts of the economy, thus hindering development of the 'industries of the future'.[11] These arguments were developed by the OECD

Secretariat in the late 1970s in the course of a series of discussions of 'positive adjustment policies'. It has been seen (in Chapter 5) that in July 1979 the OECD Ministerial Council accepted in principle that: 'Positive adjustment should rely as far as possible on market forces to encourage mobility of labour and capital to their most productive uses.'

Despite the pressures for protection in the name of 'reducing the costs of adjustment', it is widely recognised that, while protection can allow internal producers to enjoy the benefits of the Community market, it may remove the pressure to remain or become competitive in third markets. This argument against recourse to protection, however, comes into conflict with the contrary, infant-industry-type argument in favour of attempting to build up competitive activities for the future behind protective barriers. In practice, the balance between the two arguments has tended to be judged on a case-by-case basis, with political pressures influencing the outcome.

Japan and the Newly-Industrialising Countries

More fundamental than the concept of costs of adjustment is the idea that competition from countries with socio-economic structures widely different from those of Western Europe is inherently dangerous. Competition from Japan has been widely regarded as particularly damaging. In the second half of the 1970s, concern grew at the effects of competition from the newly-industrialising countries (notably South Korea, Taiwan, Hong Kong and Singapore). This led to the studies by the OECD Secretariat and by an interministerial group of officials in the United Kingdom, referred to in Chapter 5.[12]

It is not a new idea that competition from countries with very different socio-economic systems can have very damaging consequences in the industrialised countries and the idea has been further developed in a series of articles by Professor Wolfgang Hager of the European University Institute in Florence.[13] He suggests that Western European countries were able to afford shorter working hours, improved physical conditions for labour and improved social security when they had a near-monopoly in the production of relatively sophisticated industrial products, but that economic and social conditions are threatened when Japan and the newly-industrialising countries (the latter with huge reserves of cheap labour) are able to compete over an increasingly wide range of products.

The problem, as it appears to many practical men, might be described as 'the theory of the upper and nether millstone'. On this view, more and more of the present manufacturing industries of Western Europe will face increasingly severe competition from the newly-industrialising countries. The evident solution would be to move into high-technology and other skill-intensive activities; but the fear is that efforts in this direction by Community countries will be forestalled and out-competed by the United States and Japan.

Arguments along these lines often appear to rest on the elementary fallacy of 'comparative advantage in nothing'.[14] While it follows from the theory of comparative cost, however, that potential welfare in a country is increased by taking advantage of the opportunities for advantageous trade made possible by international differences in the structure of relative costs, there is nothing in the theory to prove that this policy will necessarily make a country better off than it was before or prevent it from becoming poorer. The situation of a country which loses its quasi-monopoly in a wide range of manufacturing activities is analagous to that of a country which has been receiving high prices for its mineral exports, if the development of new supplies elsewhere depresses the price. On the other hand (leaving aside for the moment the problematical infant industry argument for protection), a country in this situation will tend to be still worse off if, by protection, it loses the potential advantages of gains through trade.

The fears which have been expressed under the broad designation of 'de-industrialisation' have other aspects too. Some see dangers in the apparently growing comparative advantage of the countries of north-west Europe in many service activities. It is often suggested that the scope for productivity increases is less in services than in manufacturing. The generalisation is highly suspect and there are major dangers in the argument that the general welfare could be increased by attempting to reverse the trend by protecting manufacturing industries.

Another fear arising from the increasing competition from the newly-industrialising countries is that it is creating a huge 'underclass' of the less skilled workers, who increasingly find themselves in competition on a global scale with workers in low-wage, labour-surplus countries. This could incite governments, particularly of the left, to maintain and increase protection of activities employing the relatively unskilled. Such protection is a poor substitute for improved training; it tends to hinder transfer of labour into activities of greater economic value and it reduces total real income and hence the ability of governments to provide favourable social security benefits.

All these fears can give rise to calls for protection, either to preserve threatened activities or in an effort to nurture the industries of the future (see the discussion of man-made comparative advantage below). It should be recognised, however, that the effect of protection will almost certainly be to reduce potential aggregate welfare.

Throughout the life of the Community, Japanese policies and trading practices have been seen as presenting special problems, and this is as true today as in the past. In 1977 Commissioner Davignon was quoted as saying that Japan was a 'special case outside the framework of GATT'.[15]

In 1979, excerpts were published in the press from the celebrated Commission memorandum which described Japan as 'a country of workaholics who live in what Westerners would regard as little more than rabbit hutches'. The memorandum went on to make a further point:

> Competition from a country such as this is not easy to face by a Europe where the Protestant work ethic has been substantially eroded by egalitarianism, social compassion, environmentalism, state interventionism and a widespread belief that working hard and making money are anti-social.[16]

In earlier years, the countries of Western Europe were concerned over the large imports of highly competitive Japanese goods of various kinds. This has continued to be a concern, leading to the maintenance of restraint agreements, in particular for cars and electronic consumer goods. For ships, between 1965 and 1977 the Community put pressure on Japan to accept limitations of its share of the world market. Japanese 'targeting' of particular products and markets has been held to be especially damaging. For some products, the Japanese have been accused of dumping and protective action has been taken under the Community's anti-dumping procedures. In 1982 the Community began to threaten the Japanese with action under Article XXIII of the GATT on the grounds that Japanese practices constituted 'nullification and impairment' of the Community's rights under the Agreement.

In the early 1970s another theme began to emerge and this has remained prominent ever since: pressure on Japan to make its markets more open to goods and services from the Community and to buy particular products from the Community, notably aircraft.

At various times, representatives of the Commission and of Community governments have expressed dissatisfaction at the persistence of bilateral trade deficits with Japan. Economists argue that concentration on bilateral balances is misleading and, indeed, dangerous in a multilateral trading system. In recent years, spokesmen from the Community, as also from the United States, have complained about the persistence of large overall Japanese surpluses on trade and on the current account as a whole. In 1985 the Commission produced a report entitled *Analysis of the Relations between the Community and Japan* in which it was suggested that:

> the accumulated current account and trade imbalances, with no prospect of relief in sight, are dangerous because they threaten the whole operation of the multilateral trade and payments system.'[17]

The nature of the alleged threat was not spelt out. The suggestion may simply be that Japan's overall excess of exports over imports reduces the opportunities available to producers in the Community.

Whatever the nature of the alleged threat, there is another side to the picture which is commonly overlooked. Japanese surpluses on current account are the counterpart to an excess of savings over investment. This excess of savings has been available to offset deficits elsewhere in the world – including the large federal budget and current account deficits of the United States. If the counterbalance of the Japanese surpluses had not been available, there would have been more complaints that the United States was making undue demands on the savings of the rest of the world. It may be suspected that, even if the Japanese current account surpluses were to disappear, competition from Japanese manufactured goods would still give rise to protectionist pressures.

MAN-MADE COMPARATIVE ADVANTAGE

Another argument in favour of interventionist policies is that, to a great extent, comparative advantage in international trade is not given or inherited from the past but is largely man-made. This argument was given greater emphasis in the mid-1980s; it leads to support for government action to promote the development of man-made comparative advantage in 'foot-loose' activities.

In a recent article it was suggested that tariffs could be used to influence the location of certain industries, especially high technology industries and those where there are considerable economies of scale. The author of the article goes on to say:

> the location of industry under free trade is not uniquely determined by international differences in factor prices but instead multiple equilibria exist. . . . The emergence of new technologies not only increases the pressure for protectionist measures to distribute more evenly over time the resulting adjustment costs but also induces governments to use tariffs strategically to influence the world location pattern of the new high technology industries.[18]

Arguments along these lines have been put forward in favour of protection of relatively high technology industrial products, such as consumer electronics, on the grounds that protection will maintain the profitability of firms which have the capacity to develop and manufacture new internationally competitive products in the future. This, however, can be costly as protection or subsidisation of particular industries imposes costs on the remainder of the economy. (In practice, the threat by the United States of the imposition of countervailing duties against subsidised products pushes Community industrial support in the direction of tariffs or voluntary restraint agreements.)[19] Moreover, politicians and bureaucrats, subject to political pressures, have not in the past proved to be good at picking winners. At one time it was fashionable to point to the activities of MITI in Japan, in support of the idea of active industrial policies. Latterly, however, analyses have shown that the activities of MITI have been by no means uniformly successful. There is increasing evidence that high technology does not ensure profitability – the more so if several governments choose to support the same products.

Choice of Industrial Structure

As pointed out in earlier chapters, ministers and officials in France have not, on the whole, been influenced by the theory of comparative advantage. More important in French thinking is the idea that the country (or the Community as a whole) should choose its own economic structure and not allow this to be determined in a passive way by the pattern of international competition. There is a tendency to play down the value of gains from trade arising from international differences of comparative advantage and to stress that much comparative advantage, particularly in manufacturing, is not given but created. In the early 1980s there was an emphasis on linkages (*filières*), whereby the creation or preservation of productive capacity facilitates the creation and maintenance of capacity upstream or downstream. Such thinking ties in conveniently with the *dirigiste* approach instilled in higher officials and many politicians in the *grandes écoles* and accords with their bureaucratic and political interests.

Latterly, nevertheless, there has been increased appreciation of the part that market forces can play in bringing about needed adjustment and restructuring. Governments of both left and right have emphasised the virtues of market forces at home, but observers have noticed no significant change in French attitudes to matters of Community trade policy.

BALANCE OF PAYMENTS AND EXCHANGE-RATE STABILITY

In some Community countries in some periods, the strongest influence on trade policy has been the need to deal with acute balance-of-payments difficulties. Protection has been favoured or at least seriously considered as an alternative to devaluation or contractionary macro-economic policies. Thus in the United Kingdom in the mid-1970s, the 'New Cambridge' school of economists argued in favour of overall, non-discriminatory import restraints in order to allow the government to follow expansionary macro-economic policies without running into a balance-of-payments constraint. This idea was taken up on the left of the Labour Party. While it was resisted by the right of the party, even in the face of the balance-of-payments crisis in 1976, it appears that the pressure for import restraints reinforced protectionist policies in the 1977 extension of the MFA and, for example, on imports of certain electronic consumer goods from the Far East. The French restraint on imports of video cassette recorders from Japan in 1982 appears to have been motivated in part by a feeling that a large bilateral trade deficit with Japan was a substantial contributory element in an overall balance-of-payments problem.

The Economic Policy Committee of the European Communities has given its opinion that:

> payments disequilibria on external account cannot be cured by attempts to restore balance in bilateral trade flows, but must be

dealt with through the determination of relative exchange rates and efficient adjustment policies. In the view of the Committee, general macro-economic problems must be dealt with by coordinated demand and supply policies.[20]

Nevertheless, as a matter of practical politics, balance-of-payments problems have reinforced the tendency to use protectionist measures to deal with particular sectoral problems or pressures. The French, in particular, have argued that the effects of changes in tariffs can be swamped by unpredictable movements of exchange rates; and hence they would argue that it is not satisfactory to discuss further liberalisation of trade until effective measures have been taken to stabilise exchange rates.

The Economic Policy Committee, on the other hand, produced contrary arguments:

> Protectionist measures taken against under-valued currencies would further unsettle the international monetary system. Indeed, such policies would make it more difficult to attain a stable system where exchange rates are determined and adjusted according to the fundamental factors of the economies.[21]

The French position is a good example of a mixture of mutually-reinforcing motives. First, there is a genuine argument that large and unpredictable exchange rate changes create difficulty for trade, so there would be a case for prior action to stabilise exchange-rates – if only feasible ways of doing so could be found. Second, insistence on the exchange-rate problem could be regard as a convenient pretext for resisting pressures to roll back protection.[22] Third, there is in France a streak of anti-Americanism and dislike of the central position of the United States in the international monetary system – the 'exorbitant privilege', in President de Gaulle's term. Finally, there was the wish to use the desire of the United States Administration for a new round of multilateral trade negotiations in the GATT to put pressure on United States fiscal and monetary policies. These motives were consistent with the general attitude of the French Government which professed itself to be less impressed than other Community governments by the argument that a new round of multilateral trade negotiations would help to stave off protectionist pressures in the United States.[23]

SUMMARY

This chapter has reviewed a wide range of considerations of public policy which have been adduced in justification or explanation of Community trade policy. On one side is the body of theory in support of liberal trade and free-market policies. On the other side are various mercantilist arguments, the conservative social welfare function and arguments relating to adjustment costs, the dangers of competition from countries with conspicuously different economic and social systems, the desire to forestall foreign competition in developing industries of the future, balance-of-payments problems and exchange-rate instability.

Probably all of these ideas have exercised a certain influence at some times and in some places, even though they pull in different directions and though some of them must be regarded as erroneous or at the least highly suspect. Often, it appears that the policies followed and actions taken can be readily explained by the interplay between private, political and bureaucratic interest. The alleged considerations of policy may be rationalisations or camouflage. Ministers and officials find it necessary to advocate or justify policies in terms of the public or national good and of the means necessary to attain the desired ends. Ideas can be acts of persuasion – what Professor J.K. Galbraith called 'conditioned power'.[24] Nevertheless, even erroneous ideas may be sincerely held. There is, indeed, what may be called the phenomenon of the congenial theory: there is a natural temptation for ministers or officials to seize upon a theory which appears to provide a respectable justification for actions they wish to take for other reasons. Often, in any case, motives for particular actions are mixed, so that even the policymakers would find it difficult to say which was more important and which less.

12 Summary and Conclusions

The conclusions of this study are summarised in this final chapter, which ends with a suggestion for the improvement of policy-making, in the interests of both public welfare and good international relations.

The trade policy of the European Community is of great importance, both for the inhabitants of the Community itself and for the rest of the world. Various efforts have been made to explain the processes of decision-making in the Community and to assess the influences which have shaped policy. Given the inevitable complexity of decision-making in the Community, it is not surprising that the various attempts at explanation differ in emphasis and in their implications.

The investigation was based on a number of case studies of particular decisions on trade policy in the European Community (see Chapter 1). The main emphasis has been on various measures of protection, taken both by the Community collectively and by individual countries, though (as recalled below) account has been taken of a number of other facets of trade policy. The investigation has been concerned essentially with three types of question.

First, what are the processes by which decisions in matters of trade policy are made? Within these processes, which individuals or groups have greater influence on policy, and which less?

Second, in the shaping of policy, what has been the relative importance of:

(a) particular interests, political, bureaucratic or private;
(b) ideas of the public or national good, and of the relationship between the desired ends and the means required to achieve them.

Third, to the extent that ideas have been influential, what have these ideas been, and how well do they stand up to critical examination?

FACETS OF COMMUNITY TRADE POLICY

With other developed countries, the European Community has progressively lowered its tariffs through a series of multilateral negotiating rounds in the GATT. As tariff protection has diminished in

161

importance, however, there has been increased emphasis on restraint agreements. The GATT *Trade Policy Review* of 1991 reported:

— over 120 remaining quantitative import restrictions, most of them operated by France and Italy; this figure does not include restrictions maintained by Spain and Portugal;
— restraint agreements under the MFA for textiles and clothing;
— some 50 other restraint agreements, negotiated by the Commission for the Community as a whole, by individual member governments or by industry associations.

In addition, the Community has taken advantage of the provisions of the GATT allowing imposition of duties on imports found to be dumped or subsidised.

In spite of the provisions of the Treaty of Rome and the logic of the Community as a common market, the Commission has for long been unable to achieve a common, Community-wide import regime for some types of goods, most notably textiles and cars. However, the decision to remove all obstacles to the internal movement of goods after the end of 1992 has increased the urgency of installing common import regimes.

From about 1983, there appeared to be increased recognition that restraint agreements have the disadvantage of increasing the profits of exporters, out of which they can finance development of the competitive products of the future. In two cases, the Community increased rates of duty, but, with generally low rates of duty overall, the possibilities are limited by the GATT rule requiring compensatory reduction of duties on other products.

The Community has made rather little use of the provision for safeguard protection under Article XIX of the GATT, because of the risk of retaliatory measures authorised by the article. The Community has argued, without success up to 1992, for an interpretation of Article XIX which would allow protection to be taken on a source-selective basis, or for 'quota modulation'.

Even leaving aside export promotion and export credit policy (not covered in this work), Community trade policies have been by no means exclusively concerned with protection of domestic producers or with the removal or denial of protection (see Chapter 2). Some of the major aspects of Community trade policy in the period covered include the following:

(a) the desire to ward off threats of protection against Community exports by other countries, and notably by the United States;

(b) the wish to establish in the GATT the right to subsidise domestic industries in certain circumstances without incurring the penalty of countervailing duties on the exports of these industries;

(c) pressure on Japan to improve market access for Community goods;

(d) concern that threats of United States protection might lead to diversion of increasing amounts of Japanese goods to the European market or that the United States might secure special privileges in the Japanese market at the expense of Community exporters;

(e) pressure to see that the more advanced of the developing countries progressively assume the full obligations of membership of the GATT;

(f) resistance to what it sees as an excessively 'legalistic' approach to the GATT on the part of the United States.

ECONOMIC BACKGROUND

The making of trade policy in the second half of the 1970s and the 1980s has to be examined against the background of general economic problems, notably rises of unemployment, together with serious inflation and balance-of-payments difficulties in several countries of the Community. These problems were exacerbated, though by no means entirely caused, by the two rounds of major increases in the price of oil in 1973–4 and 1978–9. At the same time, changes in technology, in the structure of internal demand and in the pattern of international competition (including the rise of the newly-industrialising countries) necessitated massive economic restructuring (Chapter 5).

These problems do not justify some of the actions which were taken. Indeed, there are compelling arguments that resort to protection and subsidisation made the overall problems worse rather than better. Nevertheless, the perceived difficulties of the period have to be taken into account in the effort to understand why the decision-makers thought and acted as they did.

WHO MAKES POLICY?

In the attempt to determine the motives which lie behind the decisions on trade policy, it is first necessary to find out who makes the decisions; in other words, to determine what individuals or groups have the most substantial influence on policy.

The most obvious interpretation is that decision-making at the Community level is a matter of inter-governmental politics, though powers of initiative are conferred on the Commission by the founding treaties. Some analyses have suggested, however, that the nature of the Community and its institutions allows decisions to be shaped by coalitions between particular interests in the various member countries and in the Commission. Others have stressed the influence of 'élite networks' consisting of a limited number of individuals who, by implication, exercise considerable degrees of discretion in determining Community policies (Chapter 4).

The general impression from this study is that individuals concerned in the making of trade policy, at all levels, are subject to systems of checks and balances, of rewards and penalties; they can only exercise discretion within rather narrow limits. The extent to which government ministers involve themselves in details of trade policy differs from country to country, and also as between different, successive trade ministers within a single country. A senior trade official in the German Economics Ministry said that the main way in which he found out his minister's views was when he was invited to a lunch given by the minister for people from outside the ministry. This was very different from the constant exchanges, oral and in writing, between ministers and officials in British government departments. (As regards trade policy, the difference might be explained in part by the more *ad hoc* nature of decisions of trade policy in the United Kingdom.) At the other extreme from the German example, the case studies showed several instance in which heads of government themselves took a close interest in matters of trade policy.

Commission proposals may reflect pressures from various sources; but national ministers receive the credit or blame in their own countries for Community actions, and can hardly afford to allow them to pass by default. Governmental bodies – the ministerial Councils, COREPER and the other official-level committees – keep a careful watch on all matters of Community business. Representatives of private interests – EUROFER for steel, for example – may be influential, but they are influential within the limits allowed by governmental vigilance.

One point of interest, nevertheless, is the influence that can be exercised by a skilled negotiator. For example, the Commission's senior trade negotiator in Geneva is in a strong position to arrange with the representatives of the United States and other important participants an outcome which he regards as reasonably satisfactory; he may then report this to the Commission and the Article 113 Committee of national representatives as the best that is negotiable. A national official negotiating in Brussels may be in a similarly strong position to take a view on what is negotiable. While a skilled negotiator may enjoy a certain latitude and scope for initiative, however, he also needs a good sense of what is saleable to those on whose behalf he negotiates.

Without wholly discounting the influence of skilled, energetic and determined individuals in key positions, or even the role of accidents in particular cases, it is fair to conclude that policy at Community level is largely determined by bargaining or compromise between the positions separately arrived at within the various government machines (Chapter 9).

DIFFERENT COUNTRIES, DIFFERENT APPROACHES

Three chapters (6–8) examine the making of trade policy in three of the major countries of the Community, the Federal Republic of Germany, France and the United Kingdom. These countries show marked differences in the ways in which policies are made, and often in their attitudes on particular cases of trade policy.

The German authorities have followed a liberal trade approach for manufactured goods (though not for agricultural products or some services). A deliberate decision after World War II to apply free-market principles was bolstered by desire to dissociate policy both from the Nazi past and from the communism of East Germany. This approach was further validated by success in exporting manufactured goods. Successive Economics Ministers have favoured liberal international trade policies, and this approach is firmly entrenched in the Economics Ministry. Moreover, a corporatist style of decision-making, giving influence to broad-based industry associations, has operated to bolster the liberal approach, with matters of trade policy being handled as essentially technical questions.

Despite the apparent difference in approach between Germany on the one hand and France (and, to a lesser extent the United Kingdom) on the other, an ex-Commissioner has suggested that all exemplify the same rule: that governments tend to press for free trade in sectors where they feel their national producers to be particularly competitive internationally, but to desire protection where they feel that domestic producers are uncompetitive. Certainly an aspect in German thinking has been the desire of a country which has prospered on the basis of strong exports of manufactured goods to avoid protective reactions by other countries.

On several occasions, German ministers have attempted to resist protective measures by the Community, but could not muster enough votes in the Council of Ministers to block such initiatives even on the occasions when they were supported by the representatives of the Netherlands and Denmark.

In France, by contrast with Germany, the prevailing orthodoxy at any rate up to the early 1980s was interventionist, reinforced by the training received by senior officials and by many politicians in the élite training institutions. A major strain in French thinking has been that France (or the Community as a whole) should choose its own structure of economic activity and not allow this to be determined by the vicissitudes of international competition. Protectionist approaches to trade policy were in many cases the reaction to the failures of active industrial policies. The French authorities have, on occasion, shown themselves willing to flout Community rules, for example by taking unilateral steps to limit imports of textiles and clothing in 1977 and by decreeing in 1982 that imported video cassette recorders should be channelled through the customs post at Poitiers.

In 1983 there was a significant shift to a more market-oriented approach at ministerial level; but interventionist habits of thought among officials die hard and protectionist reactions are by no means a thing of the past.

In the United Kingdom, particularly in the earlier post-war years, officials were trained in a liberal economic orthodoxy and felt themselves committed to the institution and rules of the GATT. At the same time, ministers, Conservative as well as Labour, were by no means averse to interventionist industrial policies. In the mid-1970s the Labour government of the United Kingdom, beset by a serious balance of payments problem, felt itself to be 'under siege'. It nevertheless rejected the proposal for across-the-board import restraint, to a great extent on the grounds that this would certainly provoke retaliation by other countries and was incompatible with membership of the European Community. On the other hand, it was by no means averse to particular acts of protection, such as tightening up of restrictions under the Multifibre Arrangement, an industry-to-industry restraint agreement for cars, and protective measures for various consumer electronic products.

The coming to power in 1979 of a Conservative government under Margaret Thatcher at first made little difference to trade and industrial policies; but from the mid-1980s the government's professed free-market principles have had rather more influence on policy.

PLAY OF INTERESTS

Several authors have tried to explain the policy-making process in terms of the interests of the participants and the interactions between them. This, however, begs important questions about what the interests of the participants in fact are – to what extent, for example, they embrace desires to promote the public good (which in turn may be differently conceived by different participants).

One point which has emerged very clearly is the effect on policy of the desire of governments to maintain support and to be re-elected. Thus governments tend to react to private interests according to the number of votes likely to be won or lost, particularly in electoral districts where comparatively few votes can swing the balance.

Second, research has confirmed the familiar point that the interests of producers have been more influential than those of consumers or even of industrial users of imported products. Producers may be firms which can devote large resources to lobbying or which can make their views heard through industry associations. By contrast, consumers are dispersed, and may have no clear idea of the costs imposed on them by protection and subsidies.

Even when the users are other industries, there is a strong indication that their interests have often not been a significant factor in decisions on protection. Part of the explanation may be that the initiative in consideration of protection or subsidies is typically taken by politicians and officials who are concerned with firms harmed by highly competitive imports. The interests of users may then appear a somewhat secondary consideration.

Both politicians and officials tended to deny that they had been motivated by desire to bolster their positions by being seen to be active. It is nevertheless difficult to dismiss the suspicion that this has been a significant driving force, even if it appears in the actors' own minds as a desire to promote the public interest. Another argument which is difficult to pin down is that officials whose job it is to deal with particular industries are dependent on the managements in these industries for information, and need to be able to hold out the prospect of favours in return. At the least, such officials form a target for lobbying by industrial interests.

It is clear that some industry associations and even individual managements have been successful in influencing policy, but, given that witnesses have interests either in exaggerating or minimising this influence, it is difficult to judge just how much effect they have on policy or what makes a pressure group more or less effective. As broad generalisations, it appears that pressure groups tend to be effective either if they represent substantial numbers of voters, particularly in electoral districts where the outcome of the next election is uncertain, or if their aims coincide with a policy objective of the government, such as the advancement of high technology. Industry associations in areas of rapidly developing technology have advantages of superior knowledge of the technical issues. Subject to these major elements, pressure groups are also more effective the more they succeed in presenting material in forms readily usable by the officials with whom they deal.

INFLUENCE OF IDEAS

Concentration on the influence of various interests, political, bureaucratic and private, leaves aside the influence of ideas of the public good and of the relationship between desired ends and the necessary means.

The relevant ideas of the public good may be divided into two categories, those relating to the distribution of income and employment and those concerned with total potential welfare.

It has been suggested that trade policy can be explained, to a great extent at least, by the view that no substantial class in the community should suffer a large and unexpected fall in income. Such a view might appear illogical, in that it could lead to favours to people who would still remain better off at the expense of others who are worse off. On the other hand, by reducing risk it could be regarded as an element of social security giving reassurance to all.

This 'conservative social welfare function' is closely related to some of the political interests reviewed above. Governments wish to avoid losing the votes of those who are harmed by changes in the pattern of international competition, and the civil unrest which in some extreme cases has followed large job losses in particular areas. Senior officials in the Commission suggested that a certain amount of action was needed to safeguard producers hit by upsurges of imports in order to maintain public support for a generally liberal international trading system, a policy of 'bend in order not to break'.

The desire to avoid sudden, unexpected losses to substantial groups appears to have a certain value in explaining the willingness of governments to grant protection or other aids to industries hit by an upsurge of foreign competition, but it is by no means the whole of the story.

A number of other ideas, all of which have been advanced in either justification or explanation of the policies followed, are reviewed in Chapter 11 and are briefly recapitulated in the following paragraphs.

The principle of reciprocity is enshrined in the GATT and has provided the framework for trade negotiations. Insistence on reciprocity may stem from the view that the protection of other countries is particularly damaging, and possibly also that domestic protection is costless or positively beneficial. On the other hand, it also has a political basis: when governments make trade 'concessions' which remove advantages from particular sections of the population, they wish to be able to show balancing advantages, even if these do not accrue to the same people. This is one example among many of the difficulty of disentangling economic arguments and political motives.

Orthodox liberal trade theory has been influential in Germany and to some extent in the United Kingdom, but has had rather little impact on thinking in France. In opposition to this body of theory which emphasises the gains to be had from open international trade, voices in France, and Edmund Dell when he was trade minister in the United Kingdom in the mid-1970s, have stressed the desirability of independence from foreign suppliers and lenders.

Many of the ideas advanced in favour of protection spring from the view that economic restructuring is difficult and that there are costs, economic as well as social, that can be reduced by measures designed to 'buy time for adjustment'. At times of high unemployment, it is not surprising that there should be calls, reinforced by the interests of the producers themselves, to preserve existing activities for fear that they will not be replaced by new ones – the 'bird in the hand'. This attitude has been reinforced by what might be called 'sectoral blinkers' – the tendency of politicians to concentrate on the problems of textiles and clothing at one time, steel at another, cars at yet another, and so on.

Other arguments have been that competition from countries with economic and social structures very different from those of Western Europe – notably Japan and the newly-industrialising countries of South-East Asia – is in some way particularly damaging. The questions recalled in these two paragraphs raise questions of the balance between the costs of adjustment and those of non-adjustment (which may be very much higher).

In addition, the tendency of Japan to export considerably more in terms of value than it imports has been seen as restricting the opportunities available to producers in the Community. Moreover, competition from Japan and other sources is often branded as 'unfair' in terms of the GATT rules which allow increases of import duties on goods found to be dumped or subsidised. In fact, from the point of view of the population as a whole, cheap imports are a benefit, unless there is a real risk that the exporter may build up an effective monopoly and subsequently exploit it by raising prices, or unless the costs of economic restructuring are in fact high. A large part of the motive for the emphasis on 'fairness' is political, to assure those who fear the impact of foreign competition that the government has their interests at heart. Moreover, the case has been made that the Commission has been using findings of dumping as a pretext for protection in instances where there is no real case of unfairness under the GATT rules.[1] In these instances, it would seem that allegations of unfairness are being used as cover for other motives for protection.

For some industries, notably manufacture of electronic goods, protection has been advocated as a means of maintaining or building up the capacity to produce internationally competitive high-technology products – a variant on the argument for infant-industry protection.

In some Community countries in some periods, protection has been seen as a way of dealing with balance-of-payments problems. Moreover, the French authorities, in particular, have argued that further trade liberalisation was unsafe so long as there was a continuing risk of major fluctuations in exchange rates.

The ideas briefly recapitulated in the preceding paragraphs are very largely in the realm of Professor Henderson's 'do-it-yourself economics'. They ignore the fact that policies conferring benefits on particular industries impose costs, often disproportionately high, on other parts of the economy, and that protection of the industries of the past is likely to hamper the emergence of the industries of the future. Moreover, arguments based on concepts of 'market failure' tend to neglect the very real risks of political and bureaucratic failure involved in the proposed 'remedies'. (The issues are discussed in more detail in Chapter 11.)

There is an inherent difficulty, which may even be impossible to overcome in practice, of determining which of these ideas are the real motives of the policies followed and which are rationalisations of, or cover for, steps taken for reasons of political or bureaucratic interest. Clearly there is a phenomenon of the congenial theory, by which policy-makers will seize upon, and even come to believe, an apparently convincing theory which appears to justify what they want to do for other reasons.

INTERNATIONAL PRESSURES

In view of the domestic pressures and influences on member governments it is perhaps surprising that the Community is not more protectionist than it is. A major restraint on protective measures is the fear of retaliation and other damaging actions by other countries – and in particular the United States. In this connection, the Community values the GATT as an aid to the conduct of trade relations with the United States but it has resisted the development of case law through the decisions of the GATT panels.

TWO PROPOSALS

What steps should be taken to improve the making of trade policy in the European Community in the broad public (and international) interest?

In the first place, it appears anomalous that there should be no separate Council of Ministers for trade. Renato Ruggiero, as Italian trade minister, has argued that: 'The absence of an institutionalised Council of Trade Ministers has strongly affected the ability of those ministers to exercise leadership in the [Uruguay Round] negotiations.' He went on to say: 'This was very clear especially in the agricultural sector where the decisions were mainly taken by agriculture ministers.'[2]

On non-agricultural issues, however, trade ministers may themselves be unduly swayed by particular producer interests, and something more is needed to give weight to the broader public interest. To restore the balance between producers and users, measures are required:

(a) to enable and, indeed, to encourage consumers and industrial users of manufactured goods to take a full and effective part in discussions of trade and industrial policies;

(b) to this end, to generate and disseminate information both on the existence of measures of trade and industrial policy (including restraint and orderly marketing agreements) and on their economic effects; this information should cover both measures which are under consideration and those already in operation where these have considerable trade-restricting or distorting effects.

Even if the precise findings of estimates of the costs of protection and subsidisation will always be open to challenge, nevertheless the multiplication of such estimates increases the awareness of politicians, officials and the public that there *are* costs, and that these may be very large.

The need to increase knowledge of the instruments of policy and of their economic effects points to the desirability of establishing, at Community level, a body which would take evidence from representatives of consumers and users as well as from producers and unions, make the requisite economic analyses and publish the results so as to draw them to the attention of the Commission, national governments and the public. A suitable model is the Australian Industries Assistance Commission, established in 1973.[3] The findings should be published.

There would be certain advantages in establishing an institution of this kind at Community level rather than setting up a number of such bodies in the various countries of the Community. In the first place, establishment at Community level appears logical since external trade policy is supposed to be a matter of Community competence. Secondly, establishment at Community level would allow the broadest possible range of interests and economic consequences to be brought into the balance. The new body should be financed out of Community revenues. Financing should be adequate to allow it to take evidence not only at its headquarters but also in Community countries.

The new institution should be allowed to operate with complete independence. Its role in relation to the Commission and national governments should be purely advisory. Decisions on matters of trade policy would still be made by the same procedures as at present, but the decisions-makers would be supported by more thorough analysis, with less risk of bias, than is generally available to them at present. If the need is felt to take urgent action against an upsurge of imports considered to be disruptive, then such action could still be taken on a provisional basis; but there would follow a careful analysis of the pros and cons of continuing it.

Clearly, there could be objections to this proposal on grounds both of cost and of political convenience; but these objections can and should be countered. As to cost, the new body should lead to increase of economic efficiency, thus increasing economic activity and revenues by much more than would be needed to cover the cost.

At the political level, it is arguable that it suits governments to be able to dispense favours to producer interests without arousing the opposition of those who bear the costs. To this extent, increased and more effective representation of the consumer interest might be felt to make the task of government more difficult.[4] But the fate of governments depends in major degree on the general level of prosperity, however, and hence arrangements which promote economic efficiency should be valued on political grounds as well as on grounds of the public welfare which it should be the task of governments to promote. In addition, protection and subsidies are often a cause of international discord, including discord among allies. Governments are well aware of this and enter it into the balance when making decisions; but their hand would be strengthened in resisting measures which are undesirable on grounds of foreign policy if they were equipped with authoritative analyses showing that these measures are also mistaken in terms of their internal economic effects.

Appendix. Explanation of Patterns of Protection: Statistical Tests

It was mentioned in Chapter 3 that some efforts had been made to test statistically various hypotheses or models of the supply of and demand for protection. Circumstances which have been suggested as strengthening demand for, or willingness to grant, protection may be summarised as follows:

(a) ability of an industry to mobilise pressure;
(b) number of votes to be won or lost according to the support given to the industry;
(c) need to help displaced workers adjust;
(d) concern over income distribution;
(e) inability of the industry to meet foreign competition;
(f) low expectation of effective retaliation or other damaging foreign reactions.

The next step is to decide on measurable characteristics of industries which can be used in statistical tests as proxies for the circumstances suggested as being conducive to protection. In Table A1 different industry characteristics which have been used in the statistical tests reported here are set out: they show how such characteristics are supposed to relate to the various circumstances favouring protection and whether they are expected to be positively or negatively correlated with the extent of protection received.[1]

Table A2 shows the result of regression analyses made for Germany, the United Kingdom, the Netherlands and Belgium.[2] (It will be noted that none of the analyses employs by any means all of the suggested explanatory variables.) While the results for Germany and the United Kingdom correspond fairly well with the stated hypotheses, there is by no means the same correspondence in the results for the Netherlands and Belgium.

In both regressions for Germany (1972 and 1974), the number of employees in the industry and the share of domestic consumption imported are shown as positively correlated with the level of protection; the number of firms and the share of production exported are negatively correlated. All these results are in agreement with the stated hypotheses. In addition, the regression for 1972 shows a negative relationship, in accordance with the hypothesis, for value added per employee. On the other hand, in the regression for 1972, recent growth of employment in the industry is shown as positively correlated with the level of protection in contradiction of the hypothesis that protection is given to beleaguered industries. Also for 1972, the share of the four largest firms in the turnover of the industry shows a negative relationship, against the tentative hypothesis of a positive relationship. In general, though, the regression results correspond quite well with the hypotheses. (It should be noted that the regression for 1974 relates

Table A.1 Hypothesised relationships between industry characteristics and levels of or changes in protection[a]

Measurable characteristics	Circumstances favouring protection				
	Ability to mobilise pressure	Number of votes	Demands for adjustment assistance	Concern over income distribution	Inability to meet foreign competition
Concentration (share in industry turnover of four largest firms)	Positive	Negative?			
Number of firms	Negative				
Recent growth of industry turnover	Negative		Negative		
Recent growth of employment in industry	Negative		Negative		
Number of employees		Positive			
Average wage			Negative	Negative	Negative
Value added per employee			Negative	Negative	Negative
Share of domestic consumption imported	Positive				Positive
Share of production exported	Negative				Negative
Natural protection via transport costs	Negative				Negative

Source: Adapted from Robert E. Baldwin, 'Trade Policies in Developed Countries', in Ronald W. Jones and Peter B. Kenen (eds) *Handbook of International Economics*, vol. I, (Amsterdam: North-Holland, 1984).
a. Another relevant consideration, not in fact reflected in the statistical tests, is the degree of risk of damaging foreign retaliation.

Table A.2 Determinants of levels of manufacturing industry protection

Explanatory variable	Expected sign	Germany ERP 1972	Germany ERS 1974	United Kingdom D 1978	Netherlands ERP 1970	Netherlands ERP 1976	Belgium ERTP 1970
Share in industry turnover of four largest firms	+?	−	n.a.	n.a.	n.a.	n.a.	+
Number of firms	−	−**	−*	n.a.	−	−	n.a.
Recent growth of industry turnover	−	n.a.	n.a.	−	n.a.	n.a.	n.a.
Recent growth of employment in industry	−	+	+*	+	−	+**	n.a.
Number of employees	+	+	n.a.	+	−	−	n.a.
Average wage of employees	−	n.a.	n.a.	n.a.	n.a.	n.a.	−**
Value added per employee	−	−	+*	n.a.	−*	−	+**
Share of domestic consumption imported	+	+**	−*	+	−*	+	n.a.
Share of production exported	−	−**	n.a.	−	+	+	n.a.
Natural protection via transport costs	−	n.a.	n.a.	+	n.a.	n.a.	n.a.
Adjusted R²		.41	.27–.41	.46	.19	.51	.23
F – statistic		3.5	3.3–5.4	6.3	n.a.	n.a.	3.2
Number of observations		26	26	89	17	17	37

Source: Kym Anderson and Robert E. Baldwin, *The Political Market for Protection in Industrial Countries: Empirical Evidence,* Staff Working Paper No. 492 (Washington: World Bank, 1981).

Notes: ERP: effective rate of tariff and non-tariff protection and assistance. ERS: effective rate of domestic subsidy excluding EEC tariff protection. ERTP: effective rate of tariff protection. D: dummy variable (0 to 3) indicating level of effective protection. * t-value significant at 5 per cent level. ** significant at 1 per cent level.

to effective rates of domestic subsidy, excluding Community tariff protection.) The World Bank paper also shows, for Germany, a regression using the changes in manufacturing industry protection between 1964 and 1970 as the dependent variable. Rates of growth of industry turnover and average wage of employee are shown as negatively related to the increase of protection and the number of employees as positively related, all in accordance with the hypotheses.

The regression results for the United Kingdom also correspond reasonably well with the hypotheses. The number of employees in the industries and the share of domestic production imported were found to be positively correlated with the level of protection while the recent growth of industry turnover and the share of production exported were negatively correlated. On the other hand, the regressions produced the 'wrong' signs for recent growth of employment in the industry (as for Germany, 1972, and the Netherlands, 1976) and for natural protection via transport costs. (It may be that the unexpected results for growth of employment reflect the consequences rather than the causes of protection.)

By contrast with the reasonably good correspondence, for Germany and the United Kingdom, between the regression results and the hypotheses tested, the two regressions for the Netherlands show more 'wrong' than 'right' signs for the explanatory variables. That is to say, the results for the Netherlands are consistently out of line with those for Germany and the United Kingdom (and with the hypotheses) for the number of employees in the industries, the share of domestic consumption imported and the share of production exported.

The data for Belgium included only three of the explanatory variables; the 'wrong' sign (significant at the 1 per cent level) for value added per employee was obtained contrary to the results obtained for Germany (1972) and the Netherlands.

There are particular difficulties in interpreting this type of regression analysis as applied to Community countries. The common external tariff came into full force for the original six Community countries in 1968 and for the United Kingdom, Ireland and Denmark in July 1977. The common external tariff was originally fixed by an averaging process for the tariffs of Germany, France, Italy and Benelux. It may be largely for this reason that the structure of protection applying to the Netherlands largely failed to relate in the expected ways to the characteristics of the various industries in the Netherlands itself. On the other hand, some quantitative restrictions and restraint agreements (notably for textiles and clothing and cars) and some industrial subsidies, still vary from one Community country to another; these might relate to industry characteristics in the individual countries.

In analysing the structure of the common external tariff as it has emerged after the several rounds of multilateral negotiations in the GATT and other elements of protection common to all Community countries, it might appear best to refer to explanatory variables relating to the Community as a whole. This, however, would ignore the fact that maintenance of a relatively high tariff (or other Community-wide protection for, or aid to, particular types of product) may be in response to pressure from one or a few Community countries thus reflecting the circumstances in those countries.

Notes and References

Chapter 1 Importance and Complexity

1. Robert E. Baldwin, 'Trade Policies in Developed Countries', in Ronald W. Jones and Peter B. Kenen (eds) *Handbook of International Economics*, vol. I (Amsterdam: North-Holland, 1984) p. 573.
2. Throughout this book, 'Community', with initial capital, refers to the European Community of six countries from 1958 to 1972, nine from 1973 to 1980, ten from 1981 to 1985 and twelve from the beginning of 1986.
3. Source: *Direction of Trade Yearbook, 1991* (Washington: International Monetary Fund).
4. David Henderson, *1992, The External Dimension*, Occasional Papers 25 (New York: Group of Thirty, 1989). ('1992' refers to the decision in the Community to remove all internal barriers to the movement of goods and services in the Community by the end of 1992.)
5. Before the signing of the Treaty of Rome, the Treaty of Paris of 1951 had set up the European Iron and Steel Community. For administrative and decision-making purposes, the Economic Community and the Iron and Steel Community were unified in 1967.
6. Formally, the Commission is referred to as the Commission of the European Communities. Hereafter it will be referred to as the Commission.
7. Brian Hindley, 'Dumping and the Far East Trade of the European Community', *The World Economy*, vol. 11, no. 4, December 1988. Also Christopher Norall, 'New Trends in Anti-Dumping Practice in Brussels, *The World Economy*, vol. 9, no. 1, March 1986.
8. The customs union between the original six member countries was completed in 1968, and that with the United Kingdom, Ireland and Denmark in 1977.
9. R.C. Hine, *The Political Economy of European Trade: an Introduction to the Trade Policies of the EEC* (Brighton and New York: Wheatsheaf Books and St. Martin's Press, 1985) pp. 259–60.
10. Ibid., p. 260.
11. Ibid., pp. 54–5. Mentions of Germany before October 1990 refer to the Federal Republic of Germany.
12. The founding treaties are: for the European Economic Community, the Treaty of Rome of 1957; and for the Iron and Steel Community, the Treaty of Paris of 1951.
13. David Henderson, *Innocence and Design: The Influence of Economic Ideas on Policy*, British Broadcasting Corporation, 1985 Reith Lectures (Oxford: Basil Blackwell, 1986) p. 3.
14. Ibid.
15. *Agence Europe* is the name commonly given to the compilation of information and comment produced in Brussels on most days of the week by *Europe: Agence Internationale d'Information pour la Presse*.

16. Attempts to apply statistical analysis in determining the relative import-ance of various influences on trade policy have been noted, but I con-clude that there are major problems in applying such analysis to the Community. See Chapter 4 and Appendix.

Chapter 2   Principal Characteristics of Community Trade Policy

1. GATT, *Trade Policy Review: The European Communities* (Geneva: 1991).
2. Imports of many agricultural products are subject to levies under the common agricultural policy either in place of, or in addition to, the fixed tariff rates.
3. Nominal tariff rates, of course, understate the extent of tariff protection in relation to value added in production of the protected goods.
4. The original members of EFTA were Norway, Sweden, Iceland, Austria and Switzerland (together with the United Kingdom, Ireland and Portugal before their accession to the Community). Finland and Liech-tenstein joined subsequently.
5. The first Lomé Convention was negotiated in 1973 as a successor to the Yaoundé Conventions covering the former French dependencies. In addition to tariff preferences, the Lomé Conventions provide for special quotas for exports of sugar and beef from Asian, Caribbean and Pacific countries to the Community, economic aid and compensation for shortfalls of export earnings from both agricultural products and minerals.
6. The value of some preferences to Mediterranean countries may also have been eroded as a result of the accession of Spain and Portugal to the Community in 1986.
7. For a fuller account of these various preferential arrangements see GATT, op. cit.
8. The voting system is set out in the next chapter.
9. Council Regulation (EEC) 2041/68, Official Journal L303, Brussels, European Commission, 18 December 1968.
10. As a subsequent step, the list of liberalised products was further refined by transferring it from the relatively coarse tariff list (CCT) classification to the much more detailed 'Nimexe' categories. Nimexe stands for nomenclature of goods for the external trade statistics of the Community and statistics of trade between member states.
11. Council Regulation (EEC) 1439/74, *Official Journal* L159, Brussels, European Commission, 15 June 1974.
12. M.C.E.J. Bronckers, *Selective Safeguard Measures in Multilateral Trade Relations: Issues of Protectionism in GATT, European Community, and United States Law* (Deventer: Kluwer, 1985) p. 118. The reference is to case no. 41/76, *Donckerwolcke* v. *Procureur de la République, European Court Report*, p. 1921.
13. Council Regulation (EEC) 288/82, *Official Journal* L35, Brussels, Euro-pean Commission, 9 February 1982.
14. GATT, op. cit.
15. Albrecht Rothacher, *Economic Diplomacy between the European*

Community and Japan 1959–1981 (Aldershot: Gower, 1983) p. 130.
16. GATT, op. cit.
17. Ibid.
18. Ibid.
19. *Die Zeit*, 4 July 1980, cited in Rothacher, op. cit., p. 271.
20. *Agence Europe*, 14/15 February 1983.
21. For a fuller account of Community trade relations with Japan up to 1981, and the pressures from the European side, see Rothacher, op. cit.
22. Rothacher, op. cit., p. 168.
23. GATT, op. cit.
24. Article 31 of the Treaty of Rome lays down that: 'Member States shall refrain from introducing as between themselves any new quantitative restrictions or measures with equivalent effect'. There is no 'equivalent effect' clause in the Articles relating to the common commercial policy *vis-à-vis* the rest of the world. This is an example of the importance of Community law in determining what the Commission can and cannot do.
25. GATT, op. cit.
26. Ibid.
27. *Protectionism and Structural Adjustment, Statistical and Information Annex*, UNCTAD Document TD/B/1160/Add.1, (Geneva: UNCTAD Secretariat, 1988) Table 1.3.
28. GATT, op. cit., p. 18.
29. See Richard R. Rivers and John D. Greenwald, 'The Negotiation of a Code on Subsidies and Countervailing Measures: Bridging Fundamental Policy Differences', *Law and Policy in International Business*, vol. 11, 1979. Also Daniel K. Tarullo, 'The MTN Subsidies Code: Agreement without Consensus', in Seymour J. Rubin and Gary Clyde Hufbauer (eds), *Emerging Standards of International Trade and Investment: Multinational Codes and Corporate Conduct* (Totowa, NJ: Rowman & Allenhead, 1984).
30. For a detailed account of these negotiations, see Michael K. Levine, *Inside International Trade Policy Formulation: A History of the 1982 US–EC Steel Arrangements* (New York: Praeger, 1985). See also Frank Benyon and Jacques Bourgeois, 'The European Community – United States Steel Arrangement' *Common Market Law Review*, vol. 21, no. 2, June 1984, pp. 305–54.

Chapter 3   Institutional Framework of the European Community

1. The point is made by ex-Commissioner Christopher Tugendhat in *Making Sense of Europe* (Harmondsworth: Viking, 1986) p. 140.
2. Other Directorates-General which (with the relevant Commissioners) may see matters of trade policy as impinging on their subject responsibilities are:

DG IV	Competition;
DG XI	Environment, Consumer Protection and Nuclear Safety;
DG XII	Science, Research and Development;
DG XIII	Telecommunications, Information Industries and Innovation;
DG XIV	Fisheries;

DG XVI   Regional Policy;
DG XVII   Energy;
DG XXI   Customs Union and Indirect Taxation.

3. Stanley A. Budd, *The EEC: a Guide to the Maze* (Edinburgh: INRO Press, 1985) p. 16.
4. For a brief account of the role of the Parliament in the budget procedure, and of the 'cooperation procedure' in other matters, see *The Council of the European Community* (Brussels: Council of the European Communities, General Secretariat, 1990) pp. 31–9.
5. Article 144 of the Treaty of Rome.
6. *Costa* v. *ENEL*, Case 6/64, cited in Joseph Weiler, 'Community, Member States and European Integration: Is the Law Relevant?', in Loukas Tsoukalis (ed.), *The European Community, Past, Present and Future* (Oxford: Basil Blackwell, 1983) p. 43.
7. Court of Justice judgment ibid., p. 44.
8. Ibid., p. 45.
9. Budd, op. cit., p. 25.

Chapter 4   Explanations of the Process of Decision-Making

1. A. Spinelli, 'Reflections on the Institutional Crisis in the European Community', *West German Politics*, vol. 1, no. 1 (1978) p. 83. Altiero Spinelli was Commissioner in charge of industrial and technological matters from 1970 to 1976.
2. Summarised from Carole Webb, 'Introduction: Variations on a Theoretical Theme', in Helen Wallace, William Wallace and Carole Webb, *Policy-making in the European Communities* (London: John Wiley, 1977) p. 11. The functionalist view is attributed to David Mitrany in *The Functional Theory of Politics* (London: Martin Robertson, 1975).
3. Webb, op. cit.
4. R. Keohane and J. Nye, 'Transgovernmental Politics and International Organizations', *World Politics*, vol. 27, 1974, reprinted in Anthony G. McGrew and M.J. Wilson (eds) *Decision Making: Approaches and Analysis* (Manchester University Press in association with the Open University, 1982) p. 220.
5. Ibid., p. 221.
6. Glenda Goldstone Rosenthal, *The Men Behind the Decisions: Cases in European Policy-making* (Lexington, Mass.: Lexington Books, 1975).
7. Dennis C. Mueller, *Public Choice* (Cambridge University Press, 1979) p. 1.
8. For criticisms on both theoretical and empirical grounds, see B. Barry, 'The Decision to Vote', from *Sociologists, Economists and Democracy* (London: Macmillan Collier, 1970); reproduced in McGrew and Wilson (eds) op. cit., pp. 97–110.
9. Robert E. Baldwin, 'Trade Policies in Developed Countries', in Ronald W. Jones and Peter B. Kenen (eds), *Handbook of International Economics*, vol. I (Amsterdam: North-Holland, 1984) pp. 572–82.
10. A. Cawson, 'Pluralism, Corporatism and the Role of the State', *Government and Opposition*, vol. 13, no. 2, 1978; reproduced in McGrew and Wilson (eds), op. cit., p. 343.

11. McGrew and Wilson, 'Understanding Decision Making', in McGrew and Wilson (eds), op. cit., p. 13.
12. Cawson, op. cit., p. 344 in McGrew and Wilson (eds), op. cit.

Chapter 5   Economic Background to Community Trade Policy

1. Arguments in favour of interventionist policies are reviewed in Chapter 11.
2. Martin Feldstein, quoted in 'Work: The Way Ahead', *Financial Times* Special Report, 24 July 1986.
3. This was an agreement reached by the finance ministers of the so-called Group of Ten industrialised countries; the meeting was held in the Smithsonian Institution in Washington.
4. Some discipline was retained by countries, including France, which entered into the 'currency snake' arrangement with the Deutschmark, the precursor of the European Monetary System. Even within this 'Deutschmark Area', however, it was necessary to allow fairly frequent realignments of exchange rates.
5. Communiqué of the Council at Ministerial Level of the OECD, May 1974; reproduced in the *The OECD Observer*, no. 70, June 1974. Even accepting that these communiqués were drafted in the first instance by the OECD Secretariat, they were vetted by officials from member governments and may be taken as broadly reflecting the conventional wisdom (and some of the disagreements) of the time.
6. Ibid.
7. The Communiqué is reproduced in a special supplement to the *The OECD Observer*, June, 1980.
8. This concern gave rise to various official studies, notably: *The Impact of Newly Industrialising Countries on Production and Trade in Manufactures* (Paris: OECD Secretariat, 1979); and *The Newly Industrialising Countries and the Adjustment Problem*, United Kingdom Government Economic Service Working Paper no. 16, January 1979.
9. The full text is given in *GATT Activities in 1973* (Geneva: GATT Secretariat, 1974).
10. GATT, *International Trade 1976/77* (Geneva: GATT Secretariat, 1977) pp. 22–3.
11. *Agence Europe*, 7 April 1977.
12. *The OECD Observer*, no. 99, July 1979.
13. *Positive Adjustment Policies: Managing Structural Change* (Paris: OECD Secretariat, 1983) Annex B, p. 116.
14. Ibid., Annex A, p. 111.
15. *GATT Activities 1982* (Geneva: GATT Secretariat 1983).
16. *The OECD Observer*, no. 122, May 1983.
17. *The OECD Observer*, no. 129, July 1984.

Chapter 6   Making Trade Policy in Germany

1. This chapter describes developments and institutions in the Federal Republic of Germany before reunification with East Germany.

2. Government of the Federal Republic of Germany, 'Memorandum on Community Structural Policy in the Industrial Sector', reproduced in *Europe Documents*, no. 1002, 18 May 1978.
3. See Rothacher, op. cit., pp. 250 and 257.
4. See, for example, Ludwig Erhard, *Germany's Comeback to the World Market* (London: George Allen & Unwin, 1954); and *Prosperity through Competition* (London: Thames & Hudson, 1958).
5. Hugo Dicke and Hans H. Glismann, 'Industry Protection and Adjustment in West Germany: The Experience of Industries with a Self-Identified Comparative Disadvantage', paper prepared for the Institute for International Economics, Washington, November 1984.
6. Ibid.
7. Economics Ministry, *Structurbericht 1969*, BMWi-Texte no. 75, Bonn, 18 July 1969; cited in Dicke and Glismann, op. cit.
8. See John Zysman, *Governments, Markets, and Growth: Financial Systems and the Politics of Industrial Change* (Oxford: Martin Robertson, 1983) pp. 260–5.
9. *Agence Europe*, 22 August 1992.
10. G. Loewenburg, *Parliament in the German Political System* (Ithaca, NY: Cornell University Press, 1966) p. 144.
11. Simon Bulmer, *The Domestic Structure of European Policy-making in West Germany* (New York: Garland, 1986) p. 216.
12. The Coal and Steel Community is not mentioned since it was established by a *traité-loi* rather than a *traité-cadre*, giving a substantial degree of supra-national authority to its High Authority.
13. Bulmer, op. cit., pp. 227–9.
14. Ibid., p. 241.
15. Ibid., p. 108.
16. 'Social partnership and stability have been central terms in the German language of political economy: the first supported neo-corporatist ideas of collaboration in economic policy, the second was associated with the monetarist view of inflation.' Kenneth Dyson, 'Politics of Economic Recession in West Germany', in Andrew Cox (ed.), *Politics, Policy and the European Recession* (London: Macmillan, 1982) p. 36.
17. Jeremiah M. Riemer, 'West German Crisis Management: Stability and Change in the Post-Keynesian Age', in Norman J. Vig and Steven E. Schier (eds), *Political Economy in Western Democracies*, (New York: Holmes & Meier, 1985) pp. 246–7.
18. Rothacher, op. cit., p. 222.
19. Ibid., p. 267.
20. José de la Torre, *Clothing-Industry Adjustment in Developed Countries*, Thames Essay no. 38 (London: Trade Policy Research Centre, 1984) p. 157.
21. *Die Zeit*, 4 July 1980, cited in Rothacher, op. cit., p. 271.
22. Bulmer, op. cit., p. 82. These paragraphs describe arrangements in 1986.
23. Bulmer, op. cit., p. 73.

Chapter 7   Making Trade Policy in France

1. Whether this arrangement conforms with Community law depends on whether it can be regarded as an inter-industry agreement, reached and operated without intervention by the government – see Bronckers, *Selective Safeguard Measures in Multilateral Trade Relations: Issues of Protectionism in GATT, European Community, and United States Law* (Deventer: Kluwer, 1985) p. 124.
2. Bruno S. Frey, Victor Ginsburgh, Pierre Pestieau, Werner W. Pommerehne and Friedrich Schneider, 'Consensus, Dissension and Ideology among Economists in Various European Countries and in the United States', *European Economic Review*, vol. 23, 1983, pp. 59–69. The response rates ranged from 36 per cent from France (162 respondents) to 57 per cent from Germany (273 respondents).
3. Jean-Marcel Jeanneney, *Pour un Nouveau Protectionnisme* (Paris: Editions du Seuil, 1978).
4. Christian Stoffaës, *La Grande Menace industrielle* (Paris: Collection Pluriel, Calmann-Lévy, 1978).
5. François David, *Le Commerce international à la dérive* (Paris: Calmann-Lévy, 1982).
6. Jeanneney, op. cit., p. 63. (All translations from the French are mine unless otherwise indicated.)
7. Ibid., p. 66.
8. Ibid.
9. Ibid., p. 55.
10. Ibid., p. 66.
11. Ibid., pp. 66, 69.
12. Ibid., pp. 74–5.
13. Stoffaës, op. cit., pp. 425–6.
14. Ibid., p. 355.
15. Ibid., p. 470.
16. Ibid., pp. 380-1.
17. David, op. cit., pp. 14–15.
18. François Caron (translated by Barbara Bray), *An Economic History of Modern France* (London: Methuen University Paperback, 1983) pp. 366–7.
19. Ibid., p. 263. This episode is also mentioned by Stoffaës, op. cit., p. 207.
20. The *grandes écoles* are the *École Nationale d'Administration* (ENA), the *École Polytechnique* (known familiarly as the 'X', established after the Revolution in 1794), and its offshoots, the *École Nationale des Mines* and the *École Nationale des Ponts et Chaussées*.
21. Caron, op. cit., p. 364.
22. *Financial Times*, 21 May 1985; quoted in Tugendhat, *Making Sense of Europe* (Harmondsworth: Viking, 1986) p. 93.
23. J.E.S. Hayward, *Governing France: The One and Indivisible Republic*, 2nd edition (London: Weidenfeld & Nicolson, 1983) p. 21.
24. J. Zysman, *Governments, Markets and Growth: Financial Systems and the Politics of Individual Change* (Oxford: Martin Robertson, 1983) p. 106.

25. Ibid., p. 101.
26. See Zysman, op. cit., pp. 147–9.
27. 'Behind the belligerent and often caustic economic liberal rhetoric of [prime minister] Barre, lurked a powerful practice of dirigisme': Howard Machin and Vincent Wright, 'Economic Policy under the Mitterrand Presidency, 1981–1984: an Introduction', in H. Machin and V. Wright (eds), *Economic Policy and Policy-Making under the Mitterrand Presidency, 1981–1984* (London: Frances Pinter, 1985) p. 33.
28. Stoffaës, 'The Nationalizations: an Initial Assessment, 1981–1984', in Machin and Wright (eds), op. cit., pp. 160–1.
29. Laurent Fabius, Speech to the National Assembly, July 1984.
30. Hayward, op. cit., p. 4.
31. See *Financial Times Survey*, 'France', 16 June 1986.
32. *Financial Times*, 21 March 1983.
33. Hayward, op. cit., pp. 86, 113.
34. W. Safran, *The French Polity*, 2nd edn (New York, London: Longman, 1985) pp. 166–7.
35. See, for example, Frank L. Wilson, 'Les Groupes d'Intérêt sous la Cinquième République: Test de trois modèles théoriques de l'interaction entre groupes et gouvernement', *Revue Française de science politique*, vol. 33, no. 2, April 1983.
36. Hayward, op. cit., p. 113.
37. Wilson, op. cit.
38. Wilson, 'Trade Unions and Economic Policy', in Machin and Wright (eds), op. cit., p. 257.
39. Ibid.
40. Hayward, op. cit., p. 64.
41. Safran, op. cit., p. 113.
42. Ibid., p. 118.
43. Interview material.
44. See, for example, Machin and Wright, op. cit., pp. 9–13.
45. For more material on the machinery of government, see Hayward, op. cit., pp. 115–31 and 173ff.

Chapter 8 Making Trade Policy in the United Kingdom

1. Vincent Cable, *Protectionism and Industrial Decline* (London: Hodder & Stoughton, in association with the Overseas Development Institute, 1983) pp. 14–15.
2. Report of the House of Commons Industry and Trade Committee, Session 1983–84, Minutes of Evidence (London: Her Majesty's Stationery Office, 1984).
3. In 1983, the ministries of trade and industry were combined under a single Secretary of State; they had been separate departments from 1974.
4. Harold Wilson, speech to the Institute of Bankers, 16 August 1949; quoted by Paul Foot, *The Politics of Harold Wilson* (Harmondsworth: Penguin, 1968), and reproduced by Vincent Cable, op. cit., p. 10.
5. Cable, ibid.
6. Zysman, Governments, *Markets and Growth: Financial Systems and the*

Politics of Industrial Change (Oxford: Martin Robertson, 1983) p. 212.

7. Ibid., p. 216.

8. Quoted in Cable, op. cit., p. 12.

9. *Financial Times*, 26 July 1976.

10. Edmund Dell, letter to the author.

11. Edmund Dell's arguments at a fringe meeting of the Labour Party conference of 1976 were reported in *Financial Times*, 30 September 1976. He further developed his arguments in a lecture in 1977. After presenting himself as a mercantilist trade minister, he stressed the adverse foreign reactions which would follow resort to extensive import controls: 'One important interest of the strong powers is that the world should not relapse into protectionism. . . . They will have little sympathy with this country, whatever apparent short-term interests they might have, if we give an impetus to a relapse. We should not start battles we are likely to lose.' Edmund Dell, 'The Politics of Economic Interdependence', *Socialist Commentary*, April 1977.

12. *Financial Times*, 1 October 1976.

13. *Financial Times*, 14 October 1976.

14. Ibid.

15. *Industrial Policy in the European Community: Reappraisal and Priorities*, Europe Committee, Confederation of British Industry, (London: Confederation of British Industry, 1976).

16. *Financial Times*, 11 August 1976.

17. Alan Clark, *Hansard*, 13 February 1986, columns 1107 and 1108–09. The Minister for Trade is a minister of the second rank, subordinate to the Secretary of State for Trade and Industry.

18. Z.A. Silberston, *The Multi-fibre Arrangement and the UK Economy*, (London: Her Majesty's Stationery Office, 1984)

19. There were various allegations that Mrs Thatcher, as Prime Minister, filled senior positions with officials she considered to be fully sympathetic to her views. One very senior official, who had been at the centre of the government machine, discounted this view, saying that those appointed to the most senior posts would have been considered strong candidates under any government.

20. To give one example, one Deputy Secretary with responsibility for general questions of trade policy held this influential post for nine years under eight Secretaries of State, three Labour and five Conservative. In thirteen years of Conservative governments, from 1979 to 1992, there were 11 Secretaries of State for Trade (or Trade and Industry).

21. The view of the relationship between a minister and his officials as a tug-of-war has been amusingly presented in the television series and books, *Yes Minister* (followed by *Yes, Prime Minister*). Many officials dismiss the series as a travesty. Others recognise the resemblance to reality that a good caricature demands. See Jonathan Lynn and Antony Jay, *Yes Minister* (London: British Broadcasting Corporation, 1981) and subsequent volumes.

22. The existence of inter-ministerial committees, and their composition, was until recently treated as an official secret – a curious limitation on the right of citizens to know how they are governed. Nevertheless, a good

deal of material purporting to give names, composition and responsibilities of committees, even in the most sensitive areas of government, has appeared in the press.

23. Scotland is different. The Scottish Office has general coordinating powers over the whole range of government activities and it has an energetic and knowledgeable economic department. In matters of trade policy, however, the Scottish Office can only seek to influence the Department of Trade and Industry.

24. The production by an *ad hoc* inter-ministerial committee of the report, *The Newly-Industrialising Countries and the Adjustment Problem*, Government Economic Service Working Paper no. 18, (London: Her Majesty's Stationery Office, 1979) was an exceptional event. One of the ministers of the time complained that in producing a general economic analysis of the issue, the officials had in any case 'bent' their terms of reference.

25. Sir Arthur Knight, *Private Enterprise and Public Intervention: The Courtaulds Experience* (London: George Allen & Unwin, 1974) p. 101.

26. Joel Barnett, *Inside the Treasury* (London: André Deutsch, 1982) p. 133.

27. D. Marsh and W. Grant, 'Tripartism: Reality or Myth?', *Government and Opposition*, vol. 12, 1977; reproduced in McGrew and Wilson (eds), op. cit., pp. 295–6.

28. Viscount Watkinson, *Blueprint for Industrial Survival* (London: Allen & Unwin, 1976).

Chapter 9 How Decisions Are Made

1. *External Competence of the European Communities*, Select Committee on the European Communities, House of Lords, United Kingdom, Session 1984–85, (London: Her Majesty's Stationery Office, 1985) p. 9.

2. See *Agence Europe*, 27 July 1977.

3. *Agence Europe*, 14–15 December 1982.

4. *Agence Europe*, 22 February 1983.

5. Renato Ruggiero, *The Place of the GATT Trading System in the European Community's External Relations*, remarks made at a meeting at the Royal Institute of International Affairs, London, March 1991.

6. Com (85) 310 final.

7. Article 58 of the Treaty of Paris provides for the adoption of production quotas for steel if the Council declares a state of 'manifest crisis'.

8. Robin Gray, 'How Does the EC Set Trade Policy: Article 113 Committee Plays Key Role In Determining Community Position', *Europe*, September/October, 1985, p. 24.

9. Ibid.

10. Andrew Shonfield, *Europe: Journey to an Unknown Destination* (London: Allen Lane, 1973); quoted by Ralf Dahrendorf, 'The Europeanization of Europe', in Andrew J. Pierre (ed.), *A Widening Atlantic? Domestic Change and Foreign Policy* (New York: Council on Foreign Relations, 1986) p. 46.

11. J.J. Richardson and A.G. Jordan, *Governing under Pressure*, (London: Martin Robertson, 1979); reproduced in McGrew and Wilson, *Decision*

Making: Approaches and Analysis (Manchester University Press, 1982)
p. 278.
12. Gray, op. cit., p. 24.
13. Letter to the author.
14. See, for example, Tugendhat, op. cit., pp. 86–7. This pattern of behaviour can be observed, also, in other international bodies.

Chapter 10   Interests and Pressures on Policy-Makers

1. See, for example, Mancur Olson, *The Logic of Collective Action* (Cambridge, Mass.: Harvard University Press, 1965 and 1971).
2. *Europe 1992: Europe World Partner* (Brussels: European Commission,
1988). For a view on reciprocity by a former trade minister, see Edmund
Dell, 'Of Free Trade and Reciprocity', *The World Economy*, vol. 9,
no. 2, June 1986.
3. Anthony Downs, *Inside Bureaucracy* (Boston: Little, Brown, 1967)
p. 262.
4. '. . . the new administration, even with its best liberal intentions, has
found it hard to shake off the traditional penchant of French administration for *dirigisme* and state intervention', *Financial Times Survey*,
France, 16 June 1986.
5. Olson, *The Rise and Decline of Nations: Economic Growth, Stagflation
and Social Rigidities* (New Haven, Conn.: Yale University Press, 1982)
p. 70.

Chapter 11   Influence of Ideas on Trade Policy in the Community

1. Henderson, D., *Innocence and Design: The Influence of Economic Ideas
on Policy* British Broadcasting Corporation, 1985 Reith lectures (Oxford: Basil Blackwell, 1986).
2. For a systematic presentation of this body of theory, see W.M. Corden,
Trade Policy and Economic Welfare (Oxford: Clarendon Press, 1974).
Recommendations in accordance with this body of theory were set out by
the Economic Policy Committee of the European Community, *Opinion
to the Council and the Commission on the Issue of Protectionism*, Brussels, 10 March 1983, published as an appendix to Peter Rees (formerly
Minister for Trade of the United Kingdom), 'Consideration in the European Community of Trade and Finance Issues', *The World Economy*,
vol. 6, no. 3, September 1983.
3. Tugendhat, *Making Sense of Europe* (Harmondsworth: Viking, 1986)
p. 43.
4. Edmund Dell, 'The Politics of Economic Interdependence', *Socialist
Commentary*, April 1977.
5. Corden, *Trade Policy and Economic Welfare* (Oxford, Clarendon Press,
1974) p. 107.
6. Corden, *Market Disturbances and Protection: Efficiency versus the Conservative Social Welfare Function*, Discussion Paper no. 92, (Canberra:
Australian National University, 1984) p. 24.
7. Norman Tebbit, then Secretary of State for Trade and Industry, at a

dinner organised by the Trade Policy Research Centre on 28 June 1984; from the author's notes.

8. Davignon, preface to Ivo Van Bael and Jean-François Bellis, *International Trade Law and Practice of the European Community: EEC Anti-Dumping and other Trade Protection Laws* (Bicester: CCH Editions, 1985) p. iii.

9. *Communication to the Council on the Situation and Prospects of the Textile and Clothing Industries of the Community* COM (81) 388 Final (Brussels: European Commission, 1981) p. 32 of the English text.

10. Ibid., p. 29 of the English text (emphasis added).

11. See Kenneth W. Clements and Larry A. Sjaastad, *How Protection Taxes Exporters*, Thames Essay no. 39 (London: Trade Policy Research Centre, 1984).

12. See note 8 to Chapter 5.

13. Wolfgang Hager, 'Protectionism and Autonomy: How to Preserve Free Trade in Europe,' *International Affairs*, vol. 58, no. 3, Summer 1982. See also 'Industrial Policy, Trade Policy and European Social Democracy' in John Pinder (ed.) *National Industrial Strategies and the World Economy* (London: Allanheld Osmun and Croom Helm, for the Atlantic Institute of International Affairs, 1982); 'Little Europe, Wider Europe and Western Economic Cooperation', in Tsoukalis, *The European Community, Past, Present and Future* (Oxford: Basil Blackwell, 1983).

14. Many practical men still confuse comparative advantage with international differences of absolute cost levels in some sense. In fact, of course, the theory of comparative cost states that mutually beneficial trade is possible because of differences in the structure of *relative* costs of production for different goods and services, irrespective of absolute cost levels.

15. *Financial Times*, 1 July 1977; quoted in Albrecht Rothacher, *Economic Diplomacy between the European Community and Japan 1959–1981* (Aldershot: Gower, 1983) p. 236.

16. *The Guardian* and *Financial Times*, 30 March, 1979; *The Economist*, 9 April, 1979.

17. *Analysis of the Relations between the Community and Japan*, COM (85) 574 Final, (Brussels: European Commission, 1985).

18. George H. Yannapoulos, 'The European Community's Common External Commercial Policy: Internal Contradictions and Institutional Weaknesses', *Journal of World Trade Law*, vol. 19, no. 5, September/October 1985, pp. 453–4. Reference is also made in this article to A. Shaked and J. Sutton 'Natural Oligopolies and International Trade' in H. Kierzkowski (ed.) *Monopolistic Competition and International Trade*, (Oxford University Press, 1984).

19. The decisions in 1983 and 1985 to increase rates of duty on compact disc players and video cassette recorders showed some dissatisfaction with voluntary restraint agreements as the form of protection, on the grounds that these leave the quota rents in the hands of the foreign suppliers, giving them profits which they can plough back into the development of the next generation of internationally competitive products. Nevertheless, the alternative of raising rates of duty on certain products and compensating for this by lowering the rates on others, as required by the

rules of the GATT, is becoming increasingly difficult because of the progressive reductions in overall rates of duty.

20. *Opinion to the Council and the Commission on the Issue of Protectionism*, op. cit., para. 9.
21. Ibid., para. 14.
22. Under pressure from countries other than France, the Council declaration of 19 March 1985 on a new GATT round stated that: 'Results in the monetary and financial areas should be *sought in parallel with* results in the trade field' (emphasis added). Thus the French authorities, with their desire that international monetary reform should precede further trade negotiations, were in effect outvoted. This was a case where the general practice of unanimity was not applied.
23. See Edith Cresson, French Minister for Industrial Redeployment and External Trade, 'French Attitude to a New GATT Round' (edited version of an address to a dinner organised by the Trade Policy Research Centre on 17 June 1985), *The World Economy*, vol. 8, no. 3, September 1985, p. 318.
24. John Kenneth Galbraith, *The Anatomy of Power* (London: Corgi, 1985).

Chapter 12   Summary and Conclusions

1. Two articles have strongly suggested that the method of calculation used by the Commission 'will over-estimate the dumping margin by a large amount. It will also detect dumping where, by any objective criterion, no dumping has occurred': Brian Hindley, 'Dumping and the Far East Trade of the European Community', *The World Economy*, vol. 11, no. 4, December 1988, p. 447. See also Christopher Norall, 'New Trends in Anti-Dumping Practice in Brussels, *The World Economy*, vol. 9, no. 1, March 1986.
2. Ruggiero, *The Place of the GATT Trading System in the European Community's External Relations*, remarks made at a meeting at the Royal Institute of International Affairs, London, March 1991.
3. See Olivier Long et al., *Public Scrutiny of Protection: Domestic Policy Transparency and Trade Liberalization*, Special Report no. 7 (Aldershot: Gower, for Trade Policy Research Centre, 1989) pp. 38–40.
4. It is sometimes argued that clandestine methods are needed to allow governments to 'sell out' minority interests without incurring damaging opposition – an argument of 'doing good by stealth'. On the other hand, if governments may do good by stealth, they may also do harm by stealth. In democracies, the voters should have the right to know what is being done in their name, and why.

Appendix   Explanations of Patterns of Protection: Statistical Tests

1. For detailed discussions of the rationale, see Baldwin in Jones and Kenen, (eds) *Handbook of International Economics*, vol. I (Amsterdam: North-Holland, 1984); also K. Anderson and R.E. Baldwin, *The Political Market for Protection in Industrial Countries: Empirical Evidence*, Staff Working Paper no. 492 (Washington: World Bank, 1981).

2. The regression results are taken from Anderson and Baldwin, op. cit. The primary sources are:

Germany: H.H. Glismann and F.D. Weiss, *Evidence on the Political Economy of Protection in Germany*, World Bank Staff Working Paper no. 427 (Washington: World Bank, 1980)

United Kingdom: V. Cable and I. Rebelo, *Britain's Pattern of Specialisation in Manufactured Goods with Developing Countries and Trade Protection*, World Bank Staff Working Paper no. 425 (Washington: World Bank, 1980).

Netherlands: K.A. Koekkoek, J. Kol and L.B.M. Mennes, *The Political Economy of Protection: The Netherlands*, paper presented to the World Bank Workshop on Market Penetration by LDC Manufactures into Industrial Countries, Brussels, 1980.

Belgium: P.X.M. Tharakan, *Political Economy of Protection in Belgium*, World Bank Staff Working Paper no. 431 (Washington: World Bank, 1980).

Select Bibliography

This list contains the more important references cited in the text together with a number of other important works consulted by the author in the course of the investigation.

Agence Europe, (Brussels, *Agence Internationale d'Information pour la Presse*), various numbers.

Kym Anderson and Robert E. Baldwin, *The Political Market for Protection in Industrial Countries: Empirical Evidence*, Staff Working Paper no. 492 (Washington: World Bank, 1981).

Robert E. Baldwin, 'Trade Policies in Developed Countries', in Ronald W. Jones and Peter B. Kenen (eds), *Handbook of International Economics*, vol. I (Amsterdam: North-Holland, 1984).

Frank Benyon and Jacques Bourgeois, 'The European Community–United States Steel Arrangement', *Common Market Law Review*, London, vol. 21, no. 2, June 1984, pp. 305–54.

Jagdish N. Bhagwati (ed.), *Import Competition and Response* (Chicago and London: University of Chicago Press, 1982).

M.C.E.J. Bronckers, *Selective Safeguard Measures in Multilateral Trade Relations: Issues of Protectionism in GATT, European Community and United States Law* (Deventer: Kluwer, 1985).

Stanley A. Budd, *The EEC: A Guide to the Maze* (Edinburgh: INRO Press, 1985).

Simon Bulmer, *The Domestic Structure of European Policy-Making in West Germany* (New York: Garland, 1986).

Philip A. Butt, *Pressure Groups in the European Community* (London: University Association for Contemporary European Studies, 1985).

Vincent Cable, *Protectionism and Industrial Decline* (London: Hodder & Stoughton, in association with the Overseas Development Institute, 1983).

François Caron (translated by Barbara Bray), *An Economic History of Modern France* (London: Methuen University Paperback, 1983).

A. Cawson, 'Pluralism, Corporatism and the Role of the State', *Government and Opposition*, vol. 13, no. 2, 1978.

Kenneth W. Clements and Larry A. Sjaastad, *How Protection Taxes Exporters*, Thames Essay no. 39 (London: Trade Policy Research Centre, 1984.)

Industrial Policy in the European Community: Reappraisal and Priorities, Confederation of British Industry (London: CBI Publications, 1976).

International Trade Policy for the 1980s, Confederation of British Industry (London: CBI Publications, 1980).

W.M. Corden, *Trade Policy and Economic Welfare* (Oxford: Clarendon Press, 1974).

W.M. Corden, *Market Disturbances and Protection: Efficiency versus the Conservative Social Welfare Function*, Discussion Paper no. 92 (Canberra: Australian National University, 1984).

Andrew Cox (ed.) *Politics, Policy and the European Recession* (London: Macmillan, 1982).

Edith Cresson, 'French Attitude to the New GATT Round', *The World Economy*, vol. 8, no. 3, September 1985.

Ralf Dahrendorf, 'The Europeanization of Europe' in Andrew J. Pierre (ed.), *A Widening Atlantic? Domestic Changes and Foreign Policy* (New York: Council on Foreign Relations, 1986).

François David, *Le Commerce international à la dérive* (Paris: Calmann-Lévy, 1982).

Edmund Dell, 'The Politics of Economic Interdependence', Rita Hinden Memorial Lecture, *Socialist Commentary*, London, April 1977.

Edmund Dell, 'The Wistful Liberalism of Deepak Lal', *The World Economy*, vol. 2, no. 2, May 1979.

Edmund Dell, 'Trade Policy: Retrospect and Prospect', *International Affairs*, vol. 60, no. 2, Spring 1984.

Edmund Dell, 'Of Free Trade and Reciprocity', *The World Economy*, vol. 9, no. 2, June 1986.

Anthony Downs, *An Economic Theory of Democracy* (New York: Harper & Row, 1957).

Anthony Downs, *Inside Bureaucracy* (Boston: Little, Brown, 1967).

Ludwig Erhard, *Germany's Comeback to the World Market* (London: George Allen & Unwin, 1954).

Analysis of the Relationships between the Community and Japan, COM (85) 574, final (Brussels, European Commission, 1985).

Bulletin of the EEC (Brussels: European Commission), various issues.

Communication to the Council on the Situation and Prospects of the Textile and Clothing Industries of the Community, COM (81) 388, final (Brussels: European Commission, 1981).

Europe 1992: Europe World Partner (Brussels: European Commission, 1985).

Official Journal, Brussels, European Commission, various numbers.

Opinion to the Council and the Commission on the Issues of Protectionism, Economic Policy Committee of the European Community, (Brussels: European Commission, 1983), reproduced as an appendix to Peter Rees, 'Consideration in the European Community of Trade and Finance Issues', *The World Economy*, vol. 6, no. 3, September 1983.

Report of the Commission on the Communities' Anti-dumping and Anti-Subsidy Activities (Brussels: European Commission, annual).

Bruno S. Frey, Victor Ginsburgh, Pierre Pestieau, Werner W. Pommerehne and Friedrich Schneider, 'Consensus, Dissension and Ideology among Economists in Various European Countries and the United States', *European Economic Review*, vol. 23, 1983.

John Kenneth Galbraith, *The Anatomy of Power* (London: Corgi Books, 1985).

Trade Policy Review: *The European Communities* (Geneva: GATT Secretariat, 1991).

Robin Gray, 'How Does the EC Set Trade Policy: Article 113 Committee Plays Key Role in Determining Community Position', *Europe*, September/October 1985.

Wolfgang Hager, 'Protectionism and Autonomy: How to Preserve Free Trade in Europe', *International Affairs*, London, vol. 58, no. 3, 1982.

J.E.S. Hayward, *Governing France: The One and Indivisible Republic*, 2nd edition (London: Weidenfeld & Nicholson, 1983).

Brian Hindley, 'Dumping and the Far East Trade of the European Community', *The World Economy*, vol. 11, no. 4, December 1988.

Brian Hindley and Alasdair MacBean, 'Edmund Dell's Manifesto for Mercantilist Liberation', *The World Economy*, vol. 9, no. 4, December 1986.

David Henderson, *Innocence and Design: The Influence of Economic Ideas on Policy*, British Broadcasting Corporation, 1985 Reith Lectures (Oxford: Basil Blackwell, 1986).

R.C. Hine, *The Political Economy of European Trade: An Introduction to the Trade Policies of the EEC* (Brighton and New York: Wheatsheaf Books and St. Martin's Press, 1985).

Stanley Hoffman, 'Reflections on the Nation State in Western Europe Today', in Loukas Tsoukalis (ed.) *The European Community Past, Present and Future*, (Oxford: Basil Blackwell, 1983).

Minutes of Evidence House of Commons (United Kingdom) Select Committee on Trade and Industry, Sessions 1983–84 (London: Her Majesty's Stationery Office, 1984)

External Competence of the European Communities, House of Lords (United Kingdom), Select Committee on the European Communities. Session 1984–85, 16th Report (London: Her Majesty's Stationery Office, 1985).

Jean Marcel Jeanneney, *Pour un Nouveau Protectionnisme* (Paris: Editions du Seuil, 1978).

H. Kierkowski (ed.), *Monopolistic Competition and International Trade* (Oxford University Press, 1984).

R. Koehane and J. Nye, 'Transgovernmental Politics and International Organizations'. *World Politics*, vol. 27, 1974.

Deepak Lal, 'The Wistful Mercantilism of Mr Dell', *The World Economy*, vol. 1, no. 3, June 1978.

Michael K. Levine, *Inside International Trade Policy Formation: A History of the 1982 US–EC Steel Arrangements* (New York: Praeger, 1985)

G. Loewenburg, *Parliament in the German Political System* (Ithaca, NY: Cornell University Press, 1966).

Olivier Long et al., *Public Scrutiny of Protection: Domestic Policy Transparency and Trade Liberalization*, Special Report no. 7 (Aldershot: Gower, for the Trade Policy Research Centre, 1989).

Howard Machin and Vincent Wright (eds), *Economic Policy and Policy-Making under the Mitterand Presidency, 1981–1984* (London: Frances Pinter, 1985).

Anthony G. McGrew and M.J. Wilson (eds), *Decision Making: Approaches and Analysis* (Manchester University Press in association with the Open University, 1982).

Dennis C. Mueller, *Public Choice* (Cambridge University Press, 1979).

Christopher Norall, 'New Trends in Anti-dumping Practice in Brussels', *The World Economy*, vol. 9, no. 1, March 1986.

Mancur Olson, *The Logic of Collective Action* (Cambridge, Mass.: Harvard University Press, 1965 and 1971).

Mancur Olson, *The Rise and Decline of Nations: Economic Growth, Stagfla-tion and Social Rigidities* (New Haven, Conn.: Yale University Press, 1982).

Positive Adjustment Policies: Managing Structural Change (Paris: Organisa-tion for Economic Cooperation and Development, 1983).

Joan Pearce and John Sutton with Roy Batchelor, *Protectionism and Indus-trial Policy in Europe* (London: Routledge & Kegan Paul, for the Royal Institute of International Affairs, 1985).

John Pinder (ed.) *National Industrial Strategies and the World Economy* (London: Allanheld Osmun and Croom Helm, for the Atlantic Institute of International Affairs, 1982).

Derek Prag, *Lobbying the European Community* (London: European Demo-cratic Group, 1983).

J.J. Richardson and A.G. Jordan, *Governing under Pressure* (London: Martin Robertson, 1979).

F.F. Ridley (ed.) *Policies and Politics in Western Europe: The Impact of Recession* (London: Croom Helm, 1984).

Jeremiah M. Riemer, 'West German Crisis Management: Stability and Change in the Post-Keynesian Age', in Norman J. Vig and Steven E. Schier (eds) *Political Economy in Western Democracies* (New York: Holmes & Meier, 1985).

Richard R. Rivers and John D. Greenwald, 'The Negotiation of a Code on Subsidies and Countervailing Measures: Bridging Fundamental Policy Dif-ferences', *Law and Policy in International Business*, vol. 11, 1979.

Glenda Goldstone Rosenthal, *The Men Behind the Decisions: Cases in European Policy-making* (Lexington, Mass.: Lexington Books, 1975).

Albrecht Rothacher, *Economic Diplomacy between the European Commun-ity and Japan, 1959–1981* (Aldershot: Gower, 1983).

William Safran, 'Interest Groups in Three Industrial Democracies: France, West Germany and the United States', in F. Eidlin (ed.), *Constitutional Democracy: Essays in Comparative Politics* (Boulder, Col.: Westview Press, 1983).

William Safran, *The French Polity*, 2nd edition (New York, London: Long-man, 1985).

Z.A. Silberston, *The Multi-Fibre Arrangement and the UK Economy* (Lon-don: Her Majesty's Stationery Office, 1984).

Alan Sked and Chris Cook, *Post-War Britain: A Political History*, 2nd edition (Harmondsworth: Penguin, 1984).

Christian Stoffaës, *La Grande Menace industrielle* (Paris: Collection Pluriel, Calmann-Lévy, 1978).

Alastair Sutton, 'Relations between the European Community and Japan in 1982 and 1983', *Yearbook of European Law*, no. 3, 1984.

Daniel K. Tarullo, 'The MTN Subsidies Code: Agreement without Consen-sus', in Seymour J. Rubin and Gary Clyde Hufbauer (eds), *Emerging Standards of International Trade and Investment: Multinational Codes and Corporate Conduct* (Totowa, NJ: Rowman & Allanhead, 1984).

Trade Policy, Department of Trade (London: Her Majesty's Stationery Office, 1981).

Loukas Tsoukalis (ed.), *The European Community, Past, Present and Future* (Oxford: Basil Blackwell, 1983).

Christopher Tugendhat, *Making Sense of Europe* (Harmondsworth: Viking, 1986).

Protectionism and Structural Adjustment, Statistical and Information Annex, UNCTAD Document TD/B/1160/Add.1 (Geneva: UNCTAD Secretariat, 1988).

Ivo van Bael and Jean François Bellis, *International Trade Law and Practice of the European Community: EEC Anti-Dumping and other Trade Protection Laws* (Bicester: CCH Editions, 1985).

Norman J. Vig and Steven E. Schier (eds), *Political Economy in Western Democracies* (New York: Holmes & Meier, 1985).

Helen Wallace, William Wallace and Carole Webb, *Policy-Making in the European Communities* (London: John Wiley, 1977).

George H. Yannopoulous, 'The European Community's Common External Commercial Policy: Internal Contradictions and Institutional Weaknesses', *Journal of World Trade Law*, vol. 19, no. 5, September/October 1985.

John Zysman, *Governments, Markets and Growth: Financial Systems and the Politics of Industrial Change* (Oxford: Martin Robertson, 1983).

Index

United Nations Conference on Trade
and Development (UNCTAD), 13, 24
United States of America, 2, 5, 6, 18,
23, 27–31 passim, 69–71 passim, 93,
110, 126–7, 142–4 passim, 154–9
passim, 162–3, 171
Uruguay Round of trade negotiations,
5–6, 17, 28–31 passim, 37, 71–2, 88–9,
105, 123, 159, 171
users' interests, 102, 135, 141–2, 167
USSR, *see* Soviet Union

video-cassette recorders, *see* electric and
electronic products
voluntary export restraints, *see* restraint

agreements
voting in the Council, *see* qualified
majority vote

Watkinson, Viscount Harold, President,
Confederation of British Industry,
1976–77
Webb, Carole, British political scientist,
43–4
Wilson, Baron Harold, British President
of the Board of Trade, 1947–51,
Prime Minister, 1964–70, 1974–6, 108
wood, 26–7

Yugoslavia, 27–8